TABLE
OF CONTENTS

foreword

JOHN MCINERNEY
INTERIM DANIEL W. DIETRICH II, DIRECTOR
INSTITUTE OF CONTEMPORARY ART
UNIVERSITY OF PENNSYLVANIA

Deborah Anzinger's work addresses global issues that have become ever more urgent as we navigate a pandemic that is quickly defining our times. The environment, the economy, human rights, all these critical issues that Deborah addresses so powerfully are in stark relief today. Much as we seek new ways of existing in a post-covid world, Deborah's work offers alternate perspectives on existing in a complex and interconnected environment. *An Unlikely Birth* is a powerful testament to the ability of an artist to disrupt the world that is and imagine the world that could be.

I want to acknowledge and thank Danielle M. Purifoy for their insightful essay, "birthing from the bottom", and also for their ongoing dialogue with Deborah and Daniella that so deeply impacted this exhibition. The transcribed panel conversation "some thoughts on inhospitality" is an excellent document of the ways these three provocative and insightful minds worked together throughout the planning and implementation of this beautiful exhibition.

An Unlikely Birth would not have been possible without Deborah Anzinger's generous time and commitment. In my interim role as Director at ICA it has truly been a joy to have the opportunity to work with our incredible Whitney-Lauder Curatorial Fellow and architect of this exhibition, Daniella Rose King. I want to offer her our deep thanks for bringing Deborah's work to ICA and so deftly managing the development of this exhibition and the realization of both this catalog as well as the thoughtful programming and other activities surrounding its run at ICA. To that end, we also want to acknowledge the critical work done by our programming team led ably by James Britt and Tausif Noor. We'd also like to thank Sargent's Daughters NYC and their director Allegra LaViola.

Daniella was supported by ICA's peerless installation crew, led by their gentle and wise leader Paul Swenbeck, with assistance from Kat Bean, Hannah Declercq, Emily B. Elliott, Will Harris, Jake Kehs, Adam Lovitz, Julia Policastro, Jay Roselius, Lydia Smith, Sophie White, Ash Williams, and George Wisegarver. Kate Abercrombie, our registrar, worked tierlessly to get the work here and then back safely to the artist.

The lasting artifact of this exhibition — this beautiful catalog you hold in your hands — was designed by Nontsikelelo Mutiti and includes the gorgeous photography of our long term colleague Constance Mensh, and to both we are deeply indebted.

This exhibition would not have been possible without the support of our Board of Advisors and the University, including the Office of the Provost and Vice Provost Anita Allen. We would also like to acknowledge critical foundation support from the Dolfinger-McMahon Foundation and of course, the core support for the Whitney-Lauder Curatorial Fellow Program, Leonard and Judy Lauder.

acknowledgments

DANIELLA ROSE KING
WHITNEY-LAUDER CURATORIAL FELLOW
INSTITUTE OF CONTEMPORARY ART
UNIVERSITY OF PENNSYLVANIA

In the wake of my first exhibition at ICA, *The Last Place They Thought Of*, over conversations about black feminisms and geography, I had the good fortune of being introduced to Deborah Anzinger. I was immediately intrigued by her mysterious figures, forms and landscapes, and struck by the tension between a sumptuous, alluring aesthetic complicated by a critical and uncompromising vision. We met in Brooklyn and became friends on the long journey uptown to see an exhibition in Harlem. I was grateful for how she described *The Last Place They Thought Of* as a convergence. My curatorial work at ICA has, in many ways, been the coming together of concerns, ideas and people that had been percolating for years. Like the sargasso sea where the Atlantic currents flow, *Deborah Anzinger: An Unlikely Birth* was another such convergence. I am immensely grateful to Deborah for being such a generous, encouraging, challenging, and inspiring thinking partner and collaborator on this project. Working together proved to be a professional and personal highlight, founded on a deep concern for the issues at play, a mutual respect for each other, and the labor involved in realizing this project. I feel privileged to have been able to see her immensely beautiful and important work up close and share it with ICA's audiences.

Early on Deborah and I realized we had a shared love of the writings of geographer, lawyer, and writer Danielle M. Purifoy. We were delighted when she accepted our invitation to participate, and are extremely grateful for her astute, meaningful contribution to the conversation "on Inhospitality" held at ICA the day after the exhibition opened, represented in this publication as an edited transcription, as well as the stunning "birthing from the bottom" commissioned especially for this publication.

To Nontsikelelo Mutiti and her entire studio, it has been an honor and a privilege to work with you as a designer. Thank you for your intense, unmatched vision for this publication, which is itself a conceptual and material treasure.

Many thanks are due to my colleagues at ICA. To former director Amy Sadao, for supporting my vision, and to interim director John Mcinerney, for a thoughtful foreword to this publication. I am indebted to his curatorial guidance and professional support. And to my colleagues in the curatorial department Alex Klein, Meg Onli, and Caitlin Palmer, I am especially grateful for their feedback, encouragement and friendship. Thanks also to Tausif Noor and James Britt for help bringing the program "On Inhospitality" to fruition, and to Derek Rigby for seamless technical support and documentation of the event. Thanks also to other means (Gary Fogelson, Phil Lubliner, and Ryan Waller) for creating elegant interpretive materials and Constance Mensh for fabulous installation photography.

I am especially grateful to Kate Abercrombie who moved mountains to ensure the safe delivery and return of Deborah's work, as well as to Paul Swenbeck and Robert Chaney for their wisdom, guidance, and immense support and hard work to realize the exhibition.

Deborah and I would like to offer our intense gratitude to expert installation from a dream team of artists including: Kat Bean, Hannah Declercq, Emily B. Elliott, Will Harris, Jake Kehs, Adam Lovitz, Julia Policastro, Jay Roselius, Lydia Smith, Sophie White, Ash Williams, and George Wisegarver.

To friends and family who have nourished and supported us throughout this process: Sam Kingfisher, Josh Anzinger, Zoë Anzinger, Julia Phillips, Simone Leigh, Jareh Das, Amanprit Sandhu, Trista Mallory, and Jade Montserrat, we thank you.

And lastly, thank you to our own *unlikely births*, Asha and Rudy.

curatorial essay: an unlikely birth

DANIELLA ROSE KING
WHITNEY-LAUDER CURATORIAL FELLOW
INSTITUTE OF CONTEMPORARY ART
UNIVERSITY OF PENNSYLVANIA

The specter of the colonial plantation haunts the thematic landscape of the exhibition *Deborah Anzinger: An Unlikely Birth*, as well as the pages of this reader. The Caribbean plantation, site of indigenous dispossession, black enslavement, and dehumanization, latterly exported to colonies across the globe, is widely viewed as the progenitor of extractive capitalism, our contemporary social inequities, and global ecocide—the components of what scholars such as Naomi Klein and TJ Demos have termed the Capitalocene. Anzinger's visual lexicon, comprising ambiguous signs and symbols, and combining synthetic, organic, and living materials, seeks to erode many of the constructed formal and imagined boundaries between the body and the land inherent to the project of colonization, while her critical approach to the environment and its histories suggests new narrative structures, hierarchies, and visual tools for engaging and reckoning with the Capitalocene's pervasive realities and violence. In discreet and implicit modalities, the exhibition solicits attention to a continuum of reproductive exploitation spanning the "unlikely birth" of the plantation, where black procreation was abused as a tool of capitalism, to the simultaneous dependence upon and devaluation of reproductive and domestic labor essential to the project of contemporary patriarchal capitalism. Here we see how these terrible histories not only play out within critiques of environmental racism and postcoloniality, but how they congeal around and cling to our conceptions of geographical, architectural, subjective, and social space.

In Anzinger's work, the natural and the artificial often coalesce to become indistinguishable. Throughout the exhibition, the artist constructed scenes that are characteristic of our contemporary material entanglements, manifesting as wide landscapes, distilled studies, densely populated fields, and a self-contained three-dimensional environment. Flora both native to Philadelphia and from further afield are surrounded by and anchored within synthetic materials such as acrylic paint and Styrofoam, complicated by some convincing stand-ins for organic matter such as synthetic hair. Embroiled and intermingled, they trouble the viewer's notion of what is "natural," while speaking to the undeniably human origins of manufactured substances. These positionings provoke our consideration of more nuanced relationships to certain materials, reminding us of the units of plastic waste that will soon outnumber fish in the ocean, or the petroleum-derived microparticles that have entered the remotest reaches of the planet's terrains, the atmosphere, and our bodies—on a cellular level. The succulent Aloe vera (also known as Aloe Barbadensis Miller, for the botanist Philip Miller who registered the species in his own name while bioprospecting on the Caribbean island of Barbados) appears throughout the exhibition, and in the broader body of Anzinger's work. Prized for its medicinal properties and ease of growth, the aloe plant is found equally today in the interior spaces of colder climates and outdoor landscapes across the tropics. The plant's presence speaks to the *anti-geographic* character of the natural world—the boundary-defying abilities of botanicals to take root in places far from their land of origin, in which capacity they enfold the stories of great migrations, changing climates, and colonial enterprises—their botanical nomenclature revealing much about the nature of imperial biopolitics and colonial bioprospecting in the Americas. The aloe plant also figures as a metaphor for the fallacies of gender identity—it simultaneously holds qualities regarded as feminine (healing, soothing, and fleshy) and masculine (phallic, penetrative, weaponized)—and for how these binaries are ascribed to both human and nonhuman entities. Anzinger is drawn to these associations for their ambivalence, which she explores, inverts, and redeploys throughout the exhibition—proposing new utilities for otherwise tired tropes.

Anzinger's work synthesizes complex and unruly ideas of history, colonialism, power, ecology, geography, and place. Creating a visually compelling lexicon, she shrewdly deconstructs and re-presents some of these inherited ideological tropes as disembodied elements and symbols that accumulate on canvas or paper; these forms are then manifest elsewhere as sculptural works made of laser-cut mirror or painted ceramic. In this fashion, Anzinger creates new psychological terrains for the unfurling of hierarchies: of gender, race, nature—revealing how their (inherited) dynamics continue to define and govern our “person-to person and person-to-nature relationships” (Anzinger 2018). The work *An Unlikely Birth*, 2018, is a particularly potent expression of this complex interplay of ideas, forms, motifs, and approaches at work. The painting depicts an abstract Jamaican landscape, where sky and land are not separate, but intertwined and layered. Hand-painted brush strokes appear to be computer-generated; impressionistic forms gesture toward unfinished figures; fragmented and gestural bodies populate the landscape, as fleshy-toned fields of color, or abstractions of breasts, vulva, and penises. Towards the center is a form redolent of a reclining male nude, composed of greenery. It is out of this form that the landscape is born. In *An Unlikely Birth*, as Anzinger seeks to reimagine the black female body within relational schemas of subjectivity and space, she finds herself compelled to wrangle with the position of the male figure. Tellingly, it is the composition itself that offers a possible resolution; he becomes one with the landscape (as we are so often told women are)—a passive, prostrate, yet fertile conflation with the land. Working against the entrenched formal impulses that privilege extraction and exploitation, Anzinger’s aesthetic reconfiguration helps us to make a break and settle upon “more equitable paradigms for value and space” (Anzinger 2018).

In the manner of a history painting that attempts to capture an event in the process of its unfolding, *An Unlikely Birth* enacts a metaphorical and literal birth, signaling the bringing into being of new ideas, performative approaches, and visual languages. A wave of synthetic afro-kinky hair holding two live aloe plants unfurling from the canvas onto the wall, supported by a Styrofoam structure, at once brings into view the (historically dehumanized) black subject, signified by the hair, and the non-human species (aloe) we share the landscape with, a concordance that asserts the intrinsic value of both in the existing hierarchy of beings and places. After a while, the plant’s roots will grow into and anchor themselves within this material, constellating the work’s evolutive, changing nature beyond the fixed image of the moment, and suggesting potentialities for human and non-human symbiosis.

The abstraction of breasts in the top right-hand corner of the painting appears elsewhere in the exhibition as a ceramic sculpture, *Unfeed*, 2019. In *Unfeed*, the bulbous “w” manifests as one of Anzinger’s teasingly ambivalent figures; its form seems to oscillate between our slippery conceptions of human/non-human and digital/hand-drawn.

Further, its title evokes one aspect of the taxing, uncompensated reproductive labor involved in childrearing, i.e., breastfeeding. Viewed historically, the work calls forth the image of the wet nurse or lactating mother, at once an iconic figure in the historical exploitation of "the black woman's body as a fertile commodity of exchange" under transatlantic chattel slavery (McKittrick 2006, 82), and a symbolic expression of extractive practices enacted on the land and the body.

THE SPACE BETWEEN THE LEGS

Anzinger describes *Before you realized you could be seen, I watched you soaked in the shade while I was conceiving*, 2018, as the conception precedent to *An Unlikely Birth*'s labor in the aesthetic ecosystem of her exhibition. In the foreground, we see the convergence of two brown oval forms—the thighs of a reclining female figure-cum-valley where two hills meet. This space constellates as a form that the poet M. NourbeSe Philip describes as "[t]he space between the Black woman's legs," and "the fulcrum of the new world plantation," which she further characterizes as the portal to sexual and reproductive technology, violence, and pleasure. By obfuscating this site by the placement of a mirror, Anzinger disrupts, denaturalizes, and denies objectification and ownership of the image.

Anzinger, in many ways formulates a figurative, abstract, and speculative map of Philip's literary paradigm across her acrylic, mirror, and synthetic hair-on-canvas pieces. The works subvert and transgress "patriarchal, normalized gender codes (male-aggressive, female-passive, male-public, female-private) which are predicated on whiteness" (McKittrick 2006, 46–47)—and in some cases throw them out entirely. Rather than articulating the masculine presence as something that penetrates and extracts from space, Anzinger flattens it into the landscape. She invests male gendered forms with potential for fecundity and mystery. Phalluses become ambiguous, reticent, fragile, and almost flimsy—they merge with the surroundings, and become plant like. By conflating the male appendages with the landscape and nature, she not only reverses the associations—of extraction and domination—but extends and expands them. We see this most readily in *Garden*, 2018, where a whole field of genitalia spring from the ground. In *Sprout*, 2019, this form moves from the painting to four ceramic pieces that dance across the wall. In *Growth Index# 1–6*, 2019, across six small paintings, we see the distillation of forms and symbols shown elsewhere, reduced to evocative elements: orifices, mounds, sprouts, plant fronds, and hair intermingle with swathes of color that gesture toward the land, water, and bodies that populate them. With *Growth Index*, the artist mines the plasticity of language, scraping back layers of meaning and association. As with *Unfeed*, Anzinger has appropriated a term associated with capitalist and bureaucratic institutions—to describe a series of organic human/non-human specimens. In the case of *Growth Index*, a term that denotes the increase of a company's value, the artist suggests her own logic and register for determining growth and value that is far removed from that convention.

THE DISTRACTION OF SYMBOLISM AS GEOPOLITICAL BODY

Whereas elsewhere in the exhibition, "fiction and aesthetics are [shown to be] useful ideas for the transmittance of ideas" (Deborah Anzinger, unpublished interview with the author, April 25, 2019), in *The Distraction of Symbolism*, 2019, Anzinger was interested in transitioning from abstraction to reality; in creating a space where ideas became labor, and labor was essential to the functioning and fulfilment of the space. The structure built at ICA referenced a "one-room shack"; a vernacular architecture widely found throughout Jamaica as well as other geopolitical terrains suggested by the exhibition, including the rural landscapes of the Caribbean and southern United States. As such, the shack acted as both a disruption of the aesthetics of the white cube, and as a subversive occupation of the museum. Made entirely from discarded building materials including wood and tin, sourced throughout the city of Philadelphia—from previous exhibitions at ICA, the dump, and home renovation—the installation was in many ways a critique of and model for more responsible approaches to exhibition-making; itself an inherently wasteful, resource-heavy field of production.

The Distraction of Symbolism encompasses the total installation of structure, plants, lights, and generators, as well as the eponymous video Anzinger installed within the space. The seven-minute-long work was shown on a screen in front of two chairs placed above two sets of pedal-powered generators. One could also see it by peeking through a window in the structure. Anzinger shot the film at various sites in Jamaica in early 2019, including Kingston, Maroon Town, and St. Elizabeth. The audio consists of ambient sound, an individual talking about periods of water scarcity and her fears for the future, as well as a conversation between host Ka'bu Ma'at Kheru and guest Dr. Paul Ivey broadcast on the Jamaican station, Irie FM's Africa Forum show. These multiple voices are interspliced throughout the video and mention some of the intertwined geopolitical and environmental specificities of Jamaica, such as the vulnerability of the watershed, use of toxic pesticides, and the power of multinational lobbies, issues that sit at the intersection of the island's colonial legacies and the uneven burden of climate debt. The video plays with juxtaposition, inversion, and mirroring, employed formally with split and screens-within-screens, and filters that reverse the colors of the footage. Similarly, talk of water scarcity is overlaid onto footage of a pair of legs half submerged in a freshwater pool—an environmental paradox that says much about local and global struggles for water access and the health of the watershed. A subsequent split screen shows us on the one hand a sinkhole, (water again in the "wrong" place, as it were) in the middle of the road, and a deserted, half-destroyed vending machine bearing some of the lettering of Pepsi, as Dr. Ivey warns that we "worship at the altar of capitalism..." This moves quickly to a split screen showing, on the left, a lush landscape and, on the right, the artist's pregnant stomach, while we hear the words "I do not understand fully... I am focused on how I am going to take care of myself when I am older...." The potentiality signified by the landscape and unborn child is juxtaposed with an uneasy uncertainty about the future before we are moved into the next scene, driving quickly though a valley listening to the radio exchange where the pair remark that the flowery, largely symbolic promises of politicians and policymakers "will not put water in your pipe" and "I do not trust them as far as I can throw them...." The video contextualizes, historicizes, and locates the shack, alongside the exhibition's fabulistic tropical landscapes, in the real topography of the Caribbean—that is, a collection of islands and nations on the very frontlines of climate change, arrested economic development, racial capitalism, and uneven geographic distribution of resources.

By inviting the visitor inside, Anzinger sought to not only accommodate the viewer, but to put them to work, as it were, by pedaling two motors anchored to the floor to create energy to sustain the non-human life forms within. The pedals drove generators that were connected to grow lights that kept the plants alive within the artificially lit, hermetically sealed gallery space. The shack thus became a site of labor, while calling on the viewer to consider the body as technology and the bodily implications of technology. Anzinger further conflates and complicates schemas of geography and subjectivity by treating the structure itself as a body. The external "skin" of the shack is covered with the fleshy pink palette and swathes of synthetic hair that appear elsewhere in Anzinger's work, as well as the pale blue of sky and water, and the protrusion of plants that are simultaneously housed inside while also serving as a green wall of the structure. Further mimicking a body, the installation required constant care and labor in order to keep the numerous plants contained within it alive. This was performed outside of gallery hours when, out of the view of visitors, the plants were watered, and taken outside to receive fresh air and direct sunlight, weeding, and pruning. This seemingly domestic gesture—to garden, to clean, to maintain—encapsulated by the care required by the installation, calls forth the ways individuals manifest reparative and restorative land practices as a means of decolonization. Gardening, farming, growing, composting, refusing pesticides, living off and in the land, in a one-room shack perhaps, are possible strategies for remediating centuries of extraction, pollution, and estrangement from place. As such the work brings the micro- and macro politics of the capitalocene into play through attention to the various manifestations of imperialism and climate debt: naming the specifics of climate change, and giving voice to those who are already experiencing the effects of toxic soil, dwindling watersheds, waste mismanagement, and aquatic pollution. With a light hand, Anzinger cultivates an uneasy ambivalence between a space as a sanctuary, home, or shelter, and as a site of friction, action, and conflict.

CONCLUSION

This is my second exhibition at ICA. My first, titled *The Last Place They Thought Of*, was a group exhibition of four artists' work—Torkwase Dyson, Lorraine O'Grady, Jade Montserrat, and Keisha Scarville—that broadly considered how histories of racial, sexual, and economic exploitation have shaped our understanding of geography, and the realities of our environment. The solo exhibition, *Deborah Anzinger: An Unlikely Birth*, constituted a continuation and convergence of parallel and intertwined concerns, approaches, and themes. As with the work in *The Last Place They Thought Of*, Anzinger is concerned with disrupting existing relationships as they pertain to the politics of land, the body, and space; and geographical, ecological, and spatial paradigms. As Anzinger herself has written:

> "The physical structure of our world, our place within it, and the stories we create through it indicate residual syntactical relationships to space (space as in the land, and space as in raced and gendered bodies) that the project of colonialism and empire has left on culture, by shaping our person-to-person and person-to-nature relationships. In this way the aesthetics of our psychic and physical environment are molded to idealize patriarchal subject-object binaries (such as penetration of space, dominance, an ability to extract resources), and to position bodies and souls in hierarchies of value based on these concepts—all being the foundation of capitalism. The ecological paradigms and aesthetic syntax of these inherited understandings is what I attempt to erode and reshape through my current work" (Anzinger 2018).

As Danielle M. Purifoy shows us in the conversation in this volume, the "zero sum" game of extractive capitalism, as it has manifested in the Americas, ensures that for growth and development to exist *over here*, there must be extraction and pollution *over there* (Purifoy, this volume, pg 78) It is in the interest of white supremacy and neoliberal capitalism to keep existing hierarchies intact, and to continue to reproduce environmental and geographic inequities. Anzinger's paintings and installations corral materials into the uncomfortable, sometimes compromising configurations we are bound to encounter outside. Yet, alongside the damning evidence of our ecocidal condition, we also find narratives, fictions, and poetry that offer possible ways out, and through, the morass. Here organisms do more than just survive; they thrive and are transformed. The titles of her works speak to us—*I Told You*—suggesting their own innate agency, not unlike that of the nonhuman lifeforms we share the planet with. They further hint at spaces of resistance— *Inhospitable, Coy, Resonant* —reparative strategies—*Fiction as a Vessel for Reality*—double entendre—*Growth Index, Unfeed, Sprout, The Distraction of Symbolism*—and humor. How has our collective exposure to and reliance upon materials and commodities reshaped our environment and climate? Why are we unable to limit our impact and implement strategies to reverse it? Anzinger's works hint at these questions while gesturing toward more nuanced relationships between place and the human and nonhuman agents that populate them.

Anzinger shows us how to expand our understanding of gender, race, and geography, to reimagine outside the oppressive systems and architectures of contemporary life. There is an intense urgency to this project of imaginative recalibration that holds potentialities for how we might birth more sustainable, equitable, livable, and perhaps unlikely geographies and futures.

REFERENCES

Anzinger, Deborah. 2018. "About: Statement." Published October 10, 2018. http://www.deborahanzinger.com/statement.html.

McKittrick, Katherine. 2006. *Demonic Grounds: Black Women and the Cartographies of Struggle.* Minneapolis: University of Minnesota.

Philip, M. NourbeSe. 1997. "Dis Place – The Space Between", in *A Genealogy of Resistance: and Other Essays*. Toronto: Mercury Press.

"some thoughts on inhospitality", this volume, 75-104.

installation views

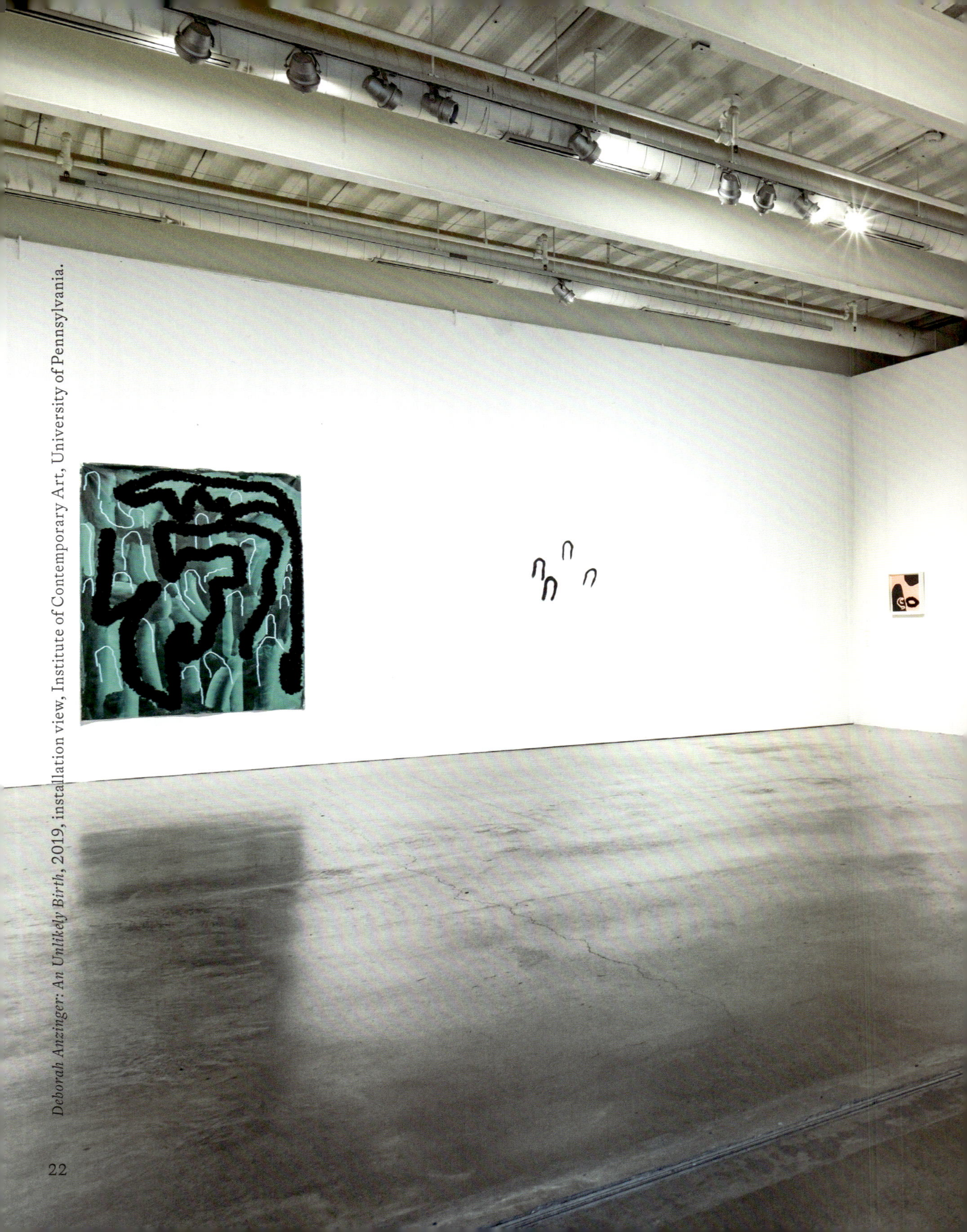

Deborah Anzinger: An Unlikely Birth, 2019, installation view, Institute of Contemporary Art, University of Pennsylvania.

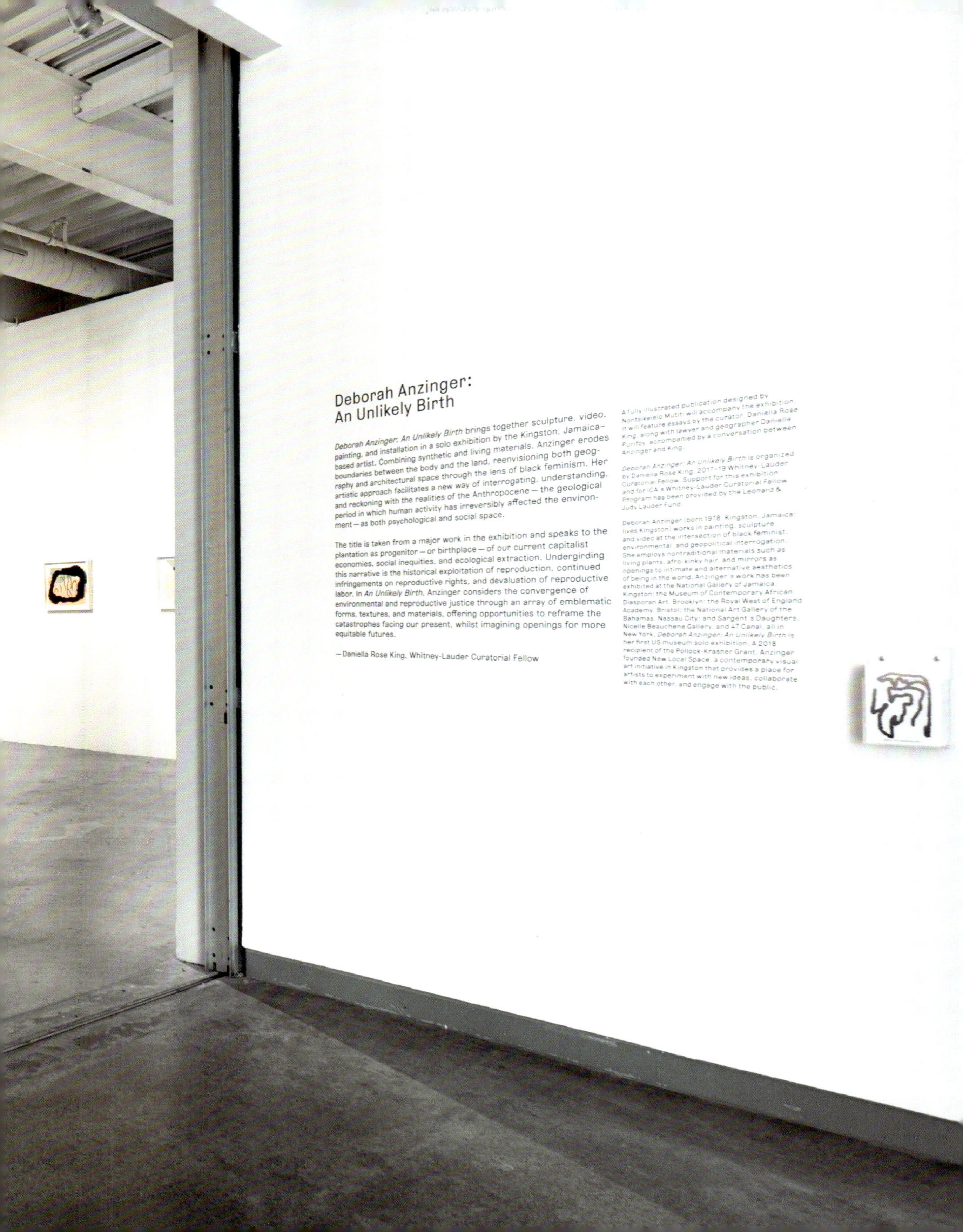
Deborah Anzinger:
An Unlikely Birth
Deborah Anzinger: An Unlikely Birth brings together sculpture, video, painting, and installation in a solo exhibition by the Kingston, Jamaica-based artist. Combining synthetic and living materials, Anzinger erodes boundaries between the body and the land, reenvisioning both geography and architectural space through the lens of black feminism. Her artistic approach facilitates a new way of interrogating, understanding, and reckoning with the realities of the Anthropocene — the geological period in which human activity has irreversibly affected the environment — as both psychological and social space.
The title is taken from a major work in the exhibition and speaks to the plantation as progenitor — or birthplace — of our current capitalist economies, social inequities, and ecological extraction. Undergirding this narrative is the historical exploitation of reproduction, continued infringements on reproductive rights, and devaluation of reproductive labor. In An Unlikely Birth, Anzinger considers the convergence of environmental and reproductive justice through an array of emblematic forms, textures, and materials, offering opportunities to reframe the catastrophes facing our present, whilst imagining openings for more equitable futures.
— Daniella Rose King, Whitney-Lauder Curatorial Fellow
A fully illustrated publication designed by Nontsikelelo Mutiti will accompany the exhibition. It will feature essays by the curator, Daniella Rose King, along with lawyer and geographer Danielle Purifoy, accompanied by a conversation between Anzinger and King.
Deborah Anzinger: An Unlikely Birth is organized by Daniella Rose King, 2017–19 Whitney-Lauder Curatorial Fellow. Support for this exhibition and for ICA's Whitney-Lauder Curatorial Fellow Program has been provided by the Leonard & Judy Lauder Fund.
Deborah Anzinger (born 1978, Kingston, Jamaica; lives Kingston) works in painting, sculpture, and video at the intersection of black feminist, environmental, and geopolitical interrogation. She employs nontraditional materials such as living plants, afro-kinky hair, and mirrors as openings to intimate and alternative aesthetics of being in the world. Anzinger's work has been exhibited at the National Gallery of Jamaica, Kingston; the Museum of Contemporary African Diasporan Art, Brooklyn; the Royal West of England Academy, Bristol; the National Art Gallery of the Bahamas, Nassau City; and Sargent's Daughters, Nicelle Beauchene Gallery, and 47 Canal, all in New York. Deborah Anzinger: An Unlikely Birth is her first US museum solo exhibition. A 2018 recipient of the Pollock-Krasner Grant, Anzinger founded New Local Space, a contemporary visual art initiative in Kingston that provides a place for artists to experiment with new ideas, collaborate with each other, and engage with the public.

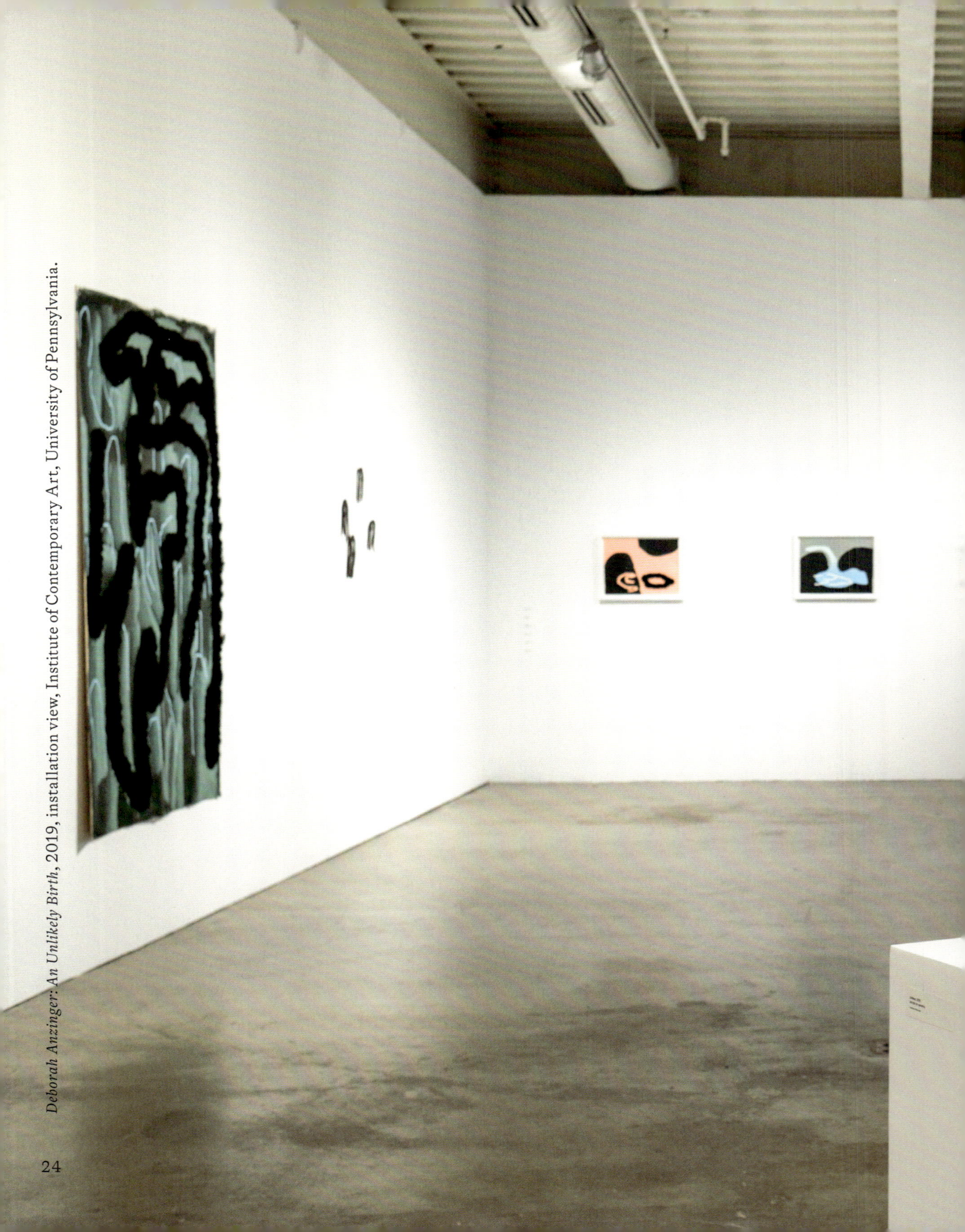

Deborah Anzinger: An Unlikely Birth, 2019, installation view, Institute of Contemporary Art, University of Pennsylvania.

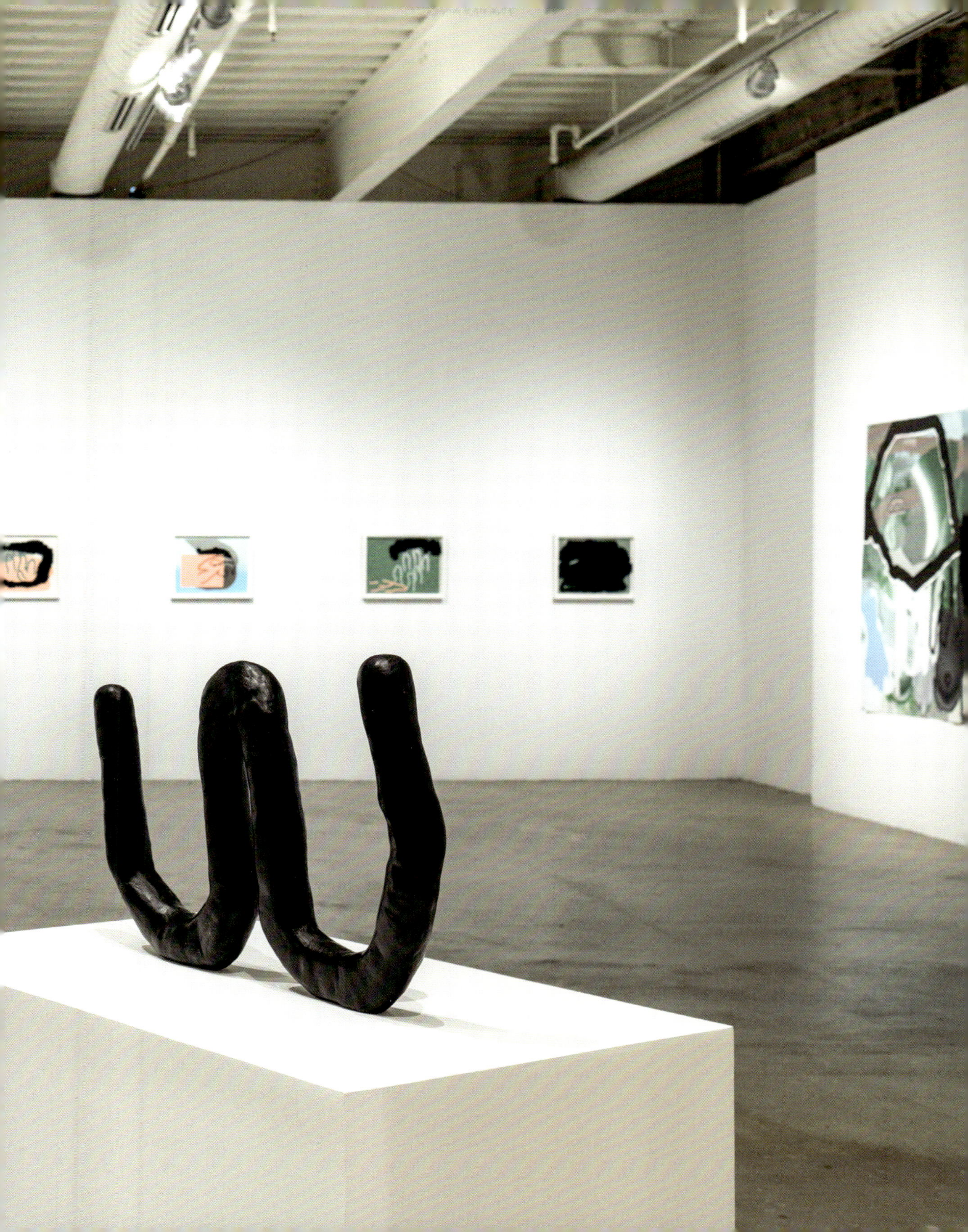

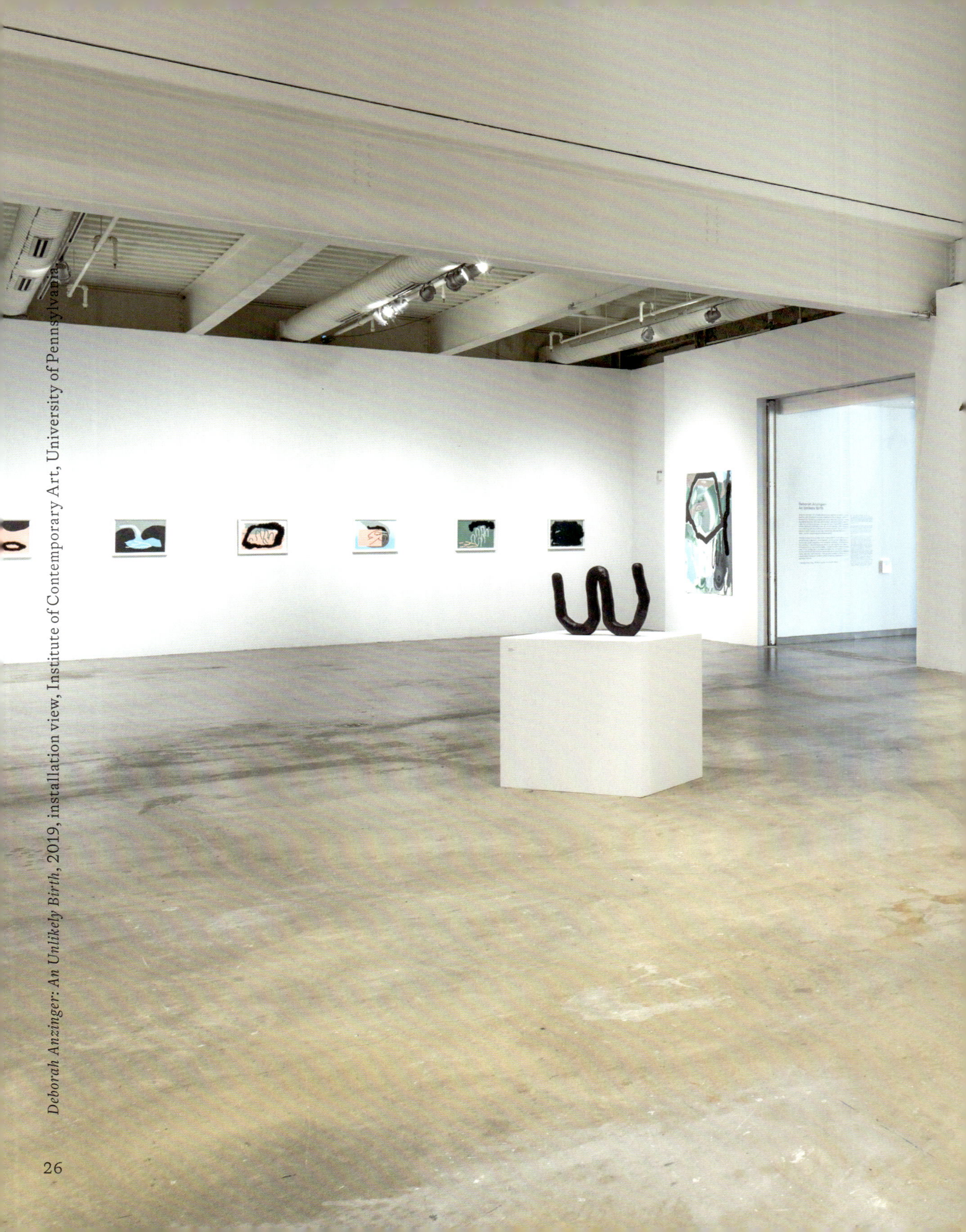

Deborah Anzinger: An Unlikely Birth, 2019, installation view, Institute of Contemporary Art, University of Pennsylvania

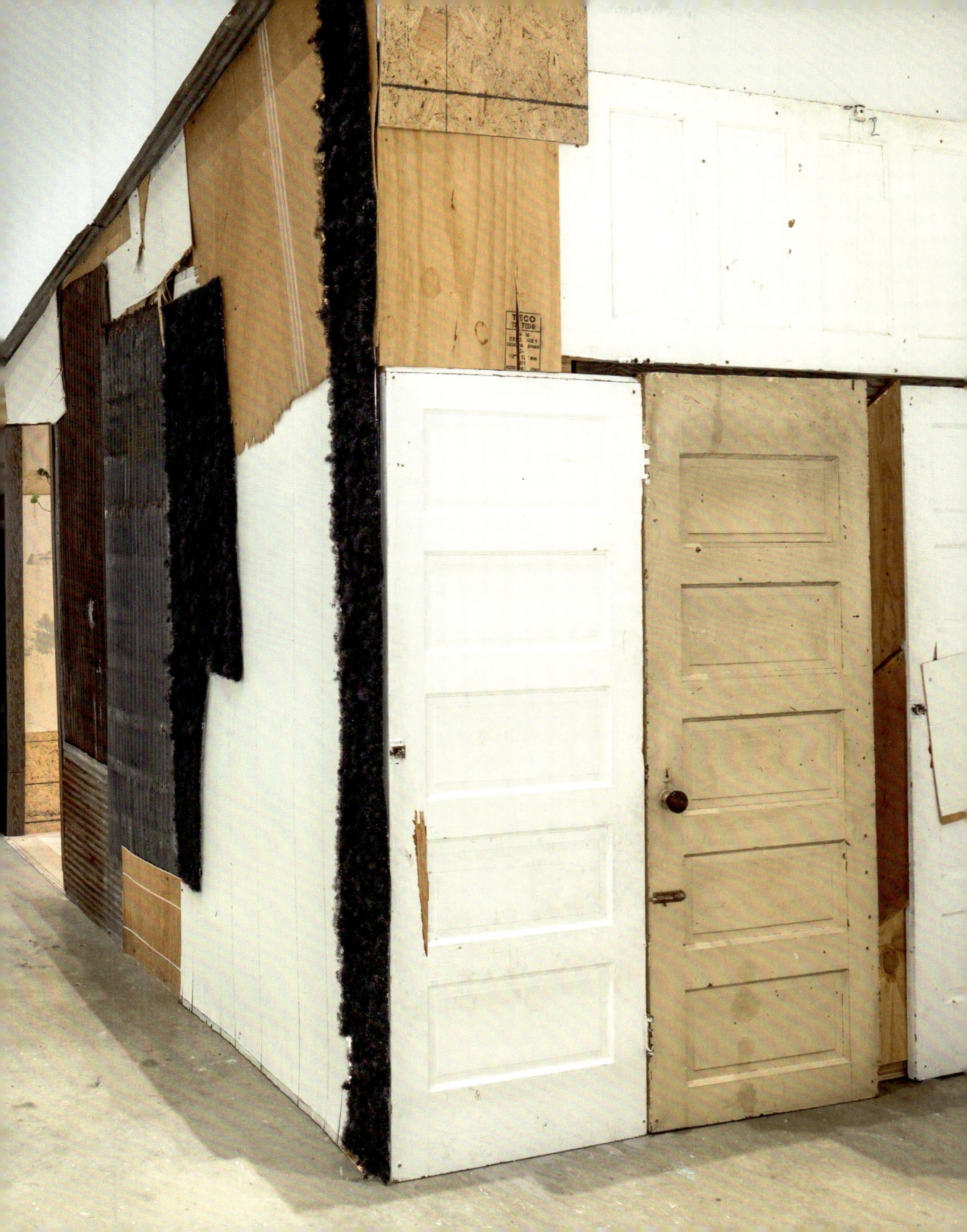
TECO

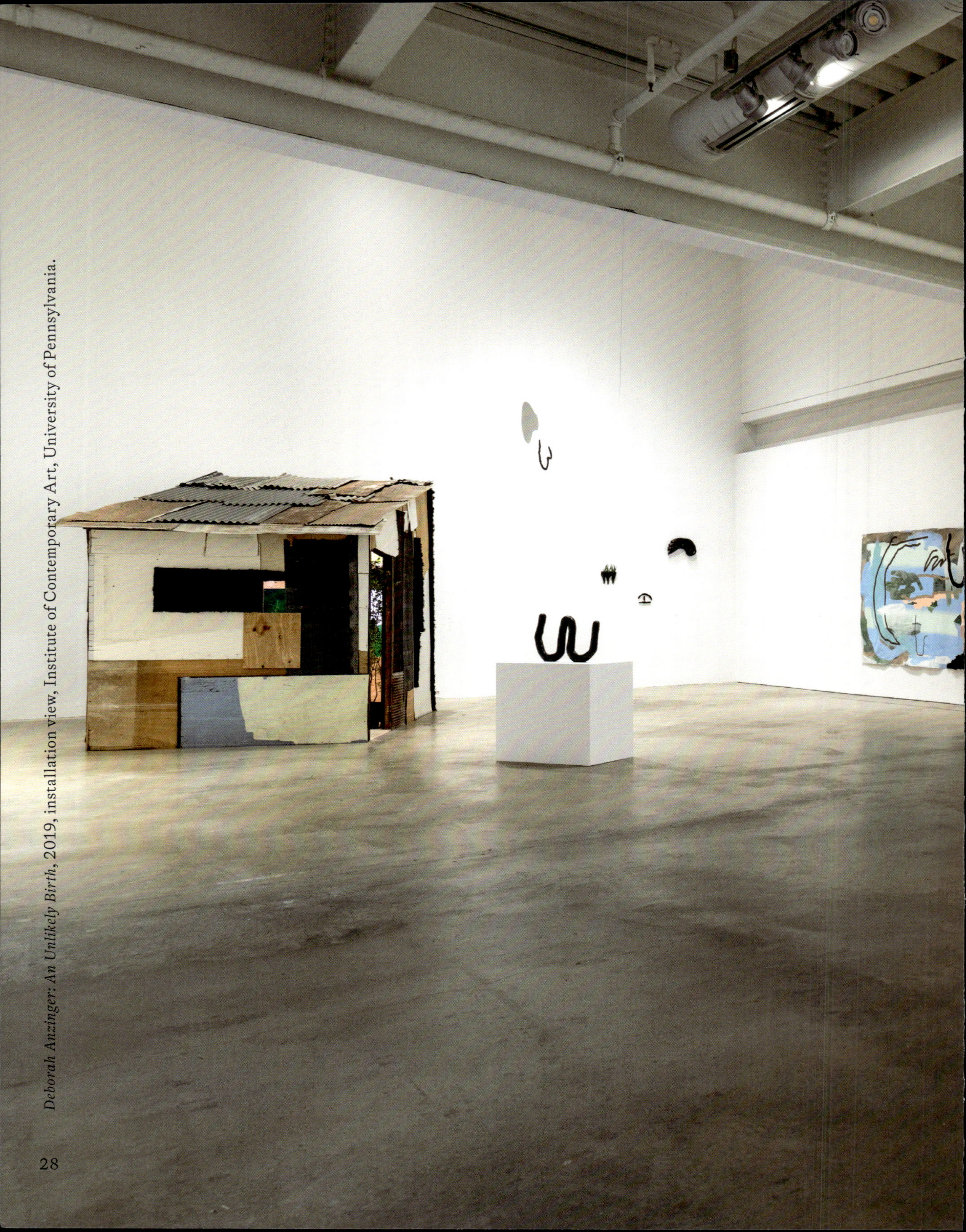

Deborah Anzinger: An Unlikely Birth, 2019, installation view, Institute of Contemporary Art, University of Pennsylvania.

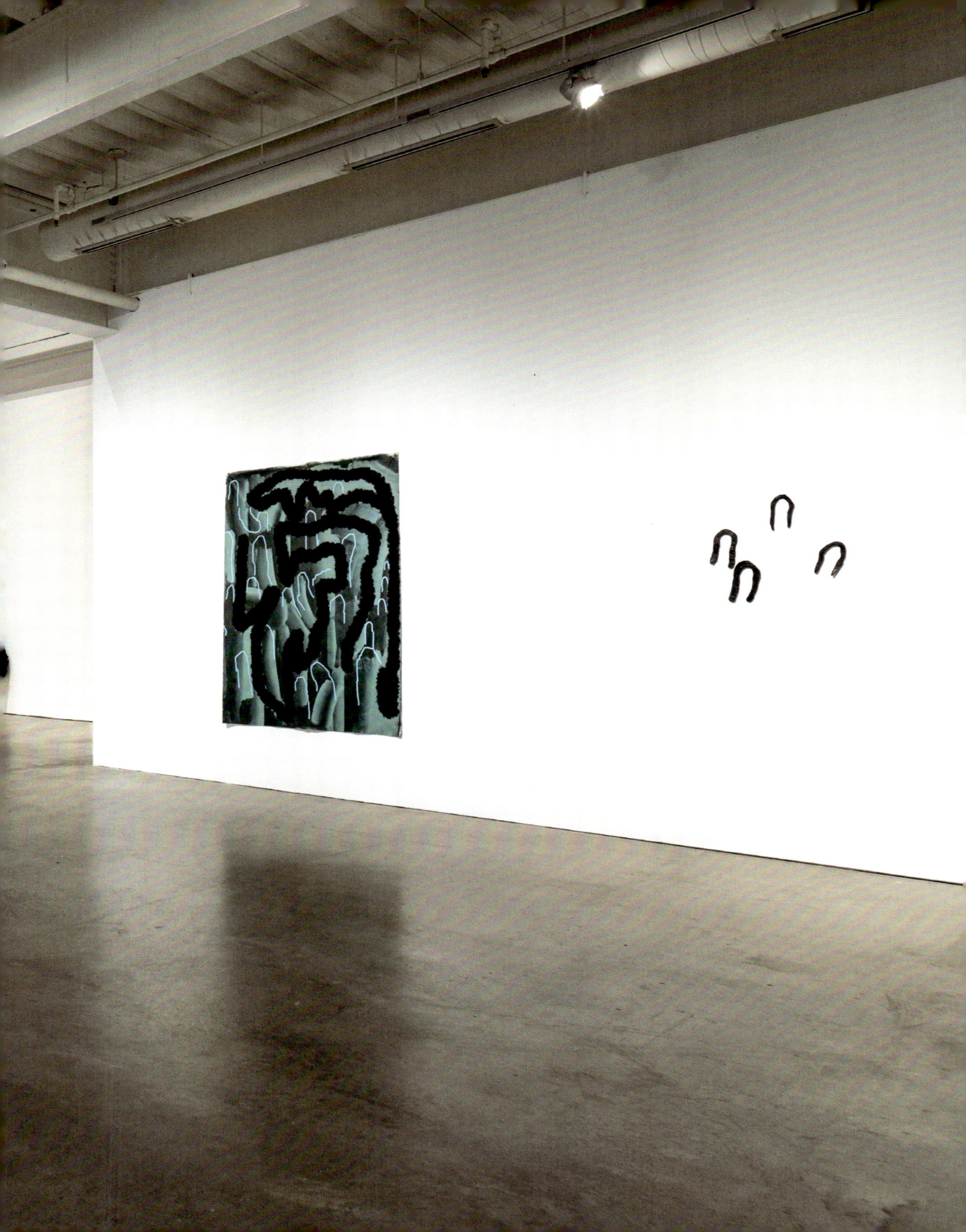

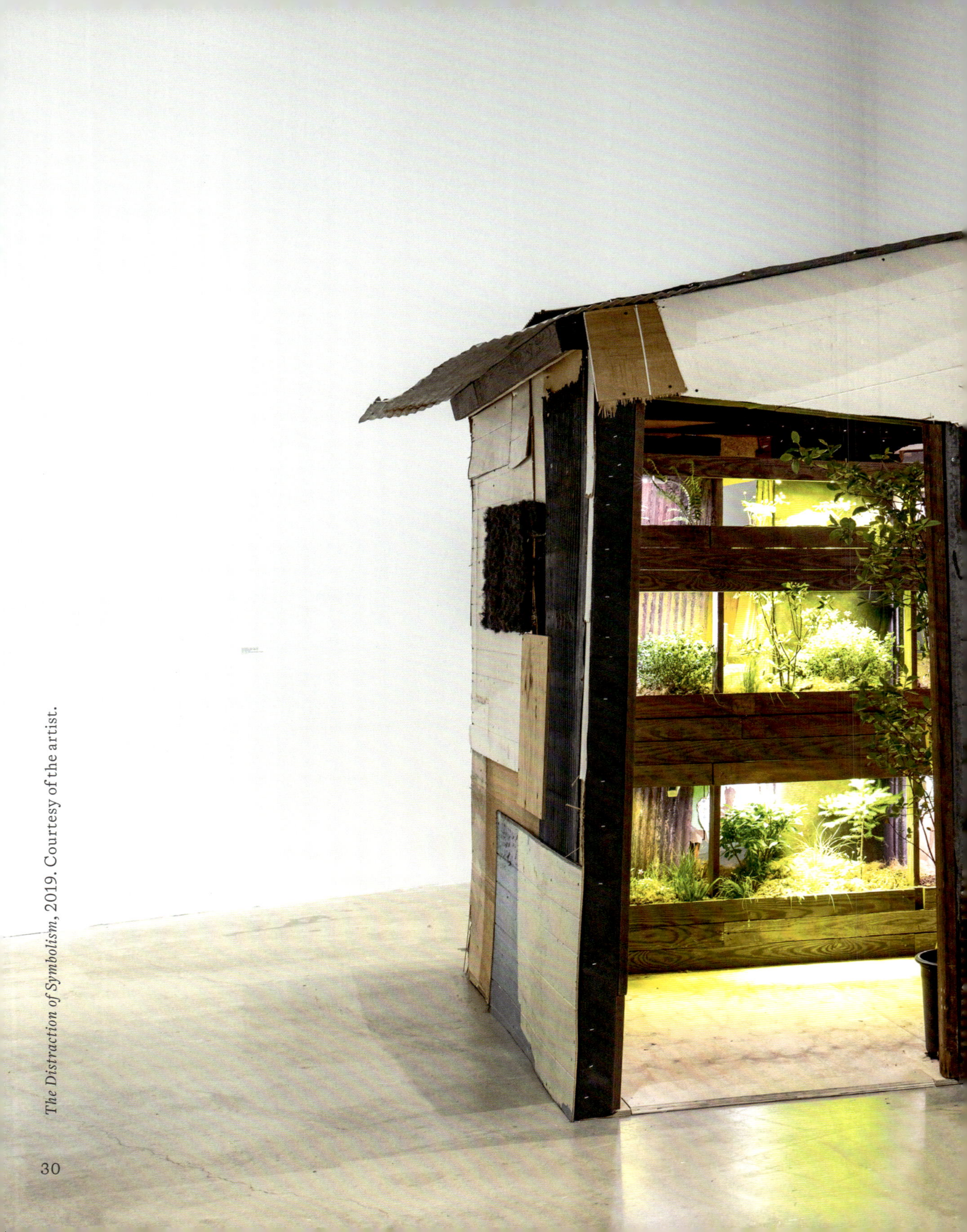

The Distraction of Symbolism, 2019. Courtesy of the artist.

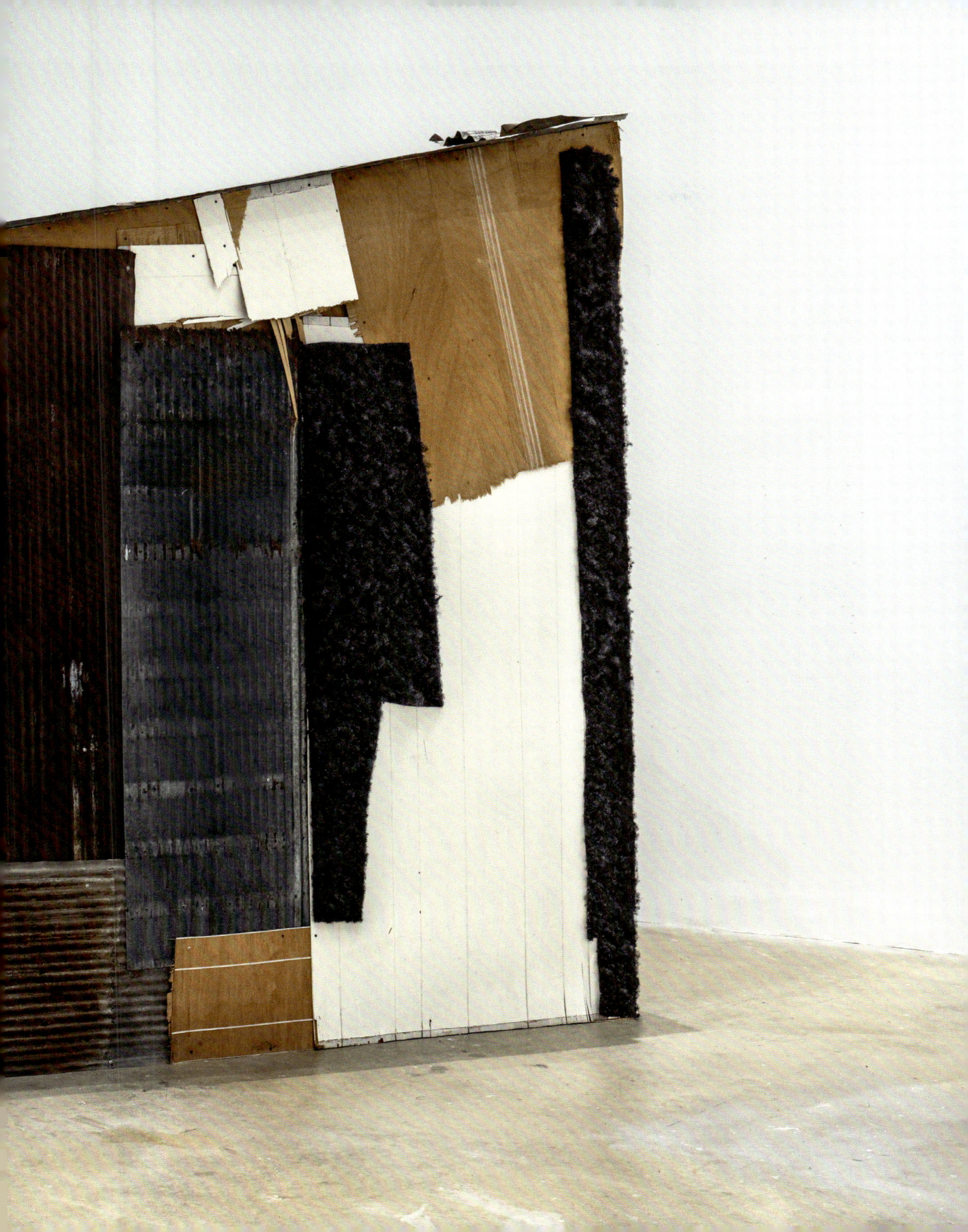

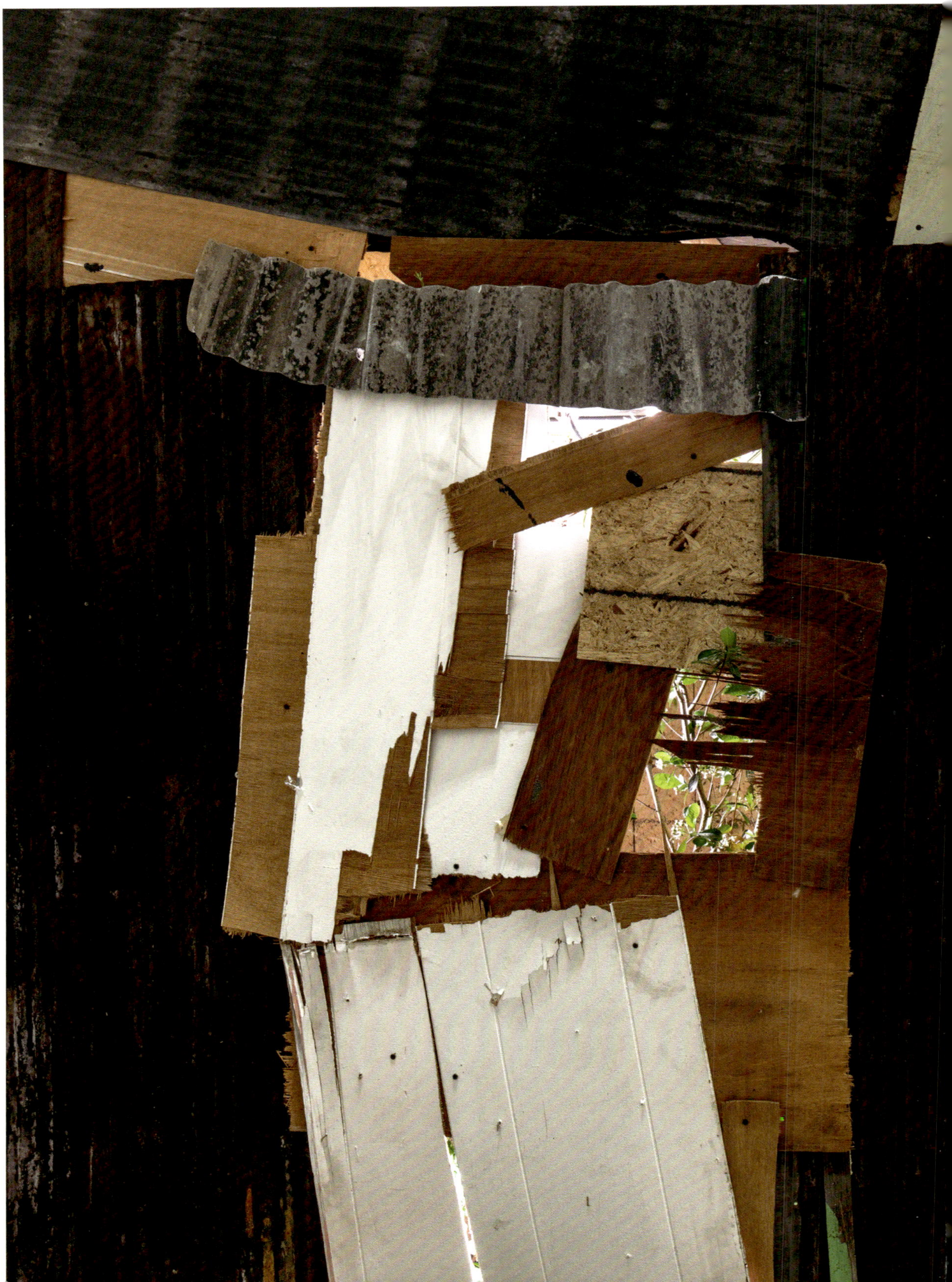

The Distraction of Symbolism (detail), 2019. Courtesy of the artist.

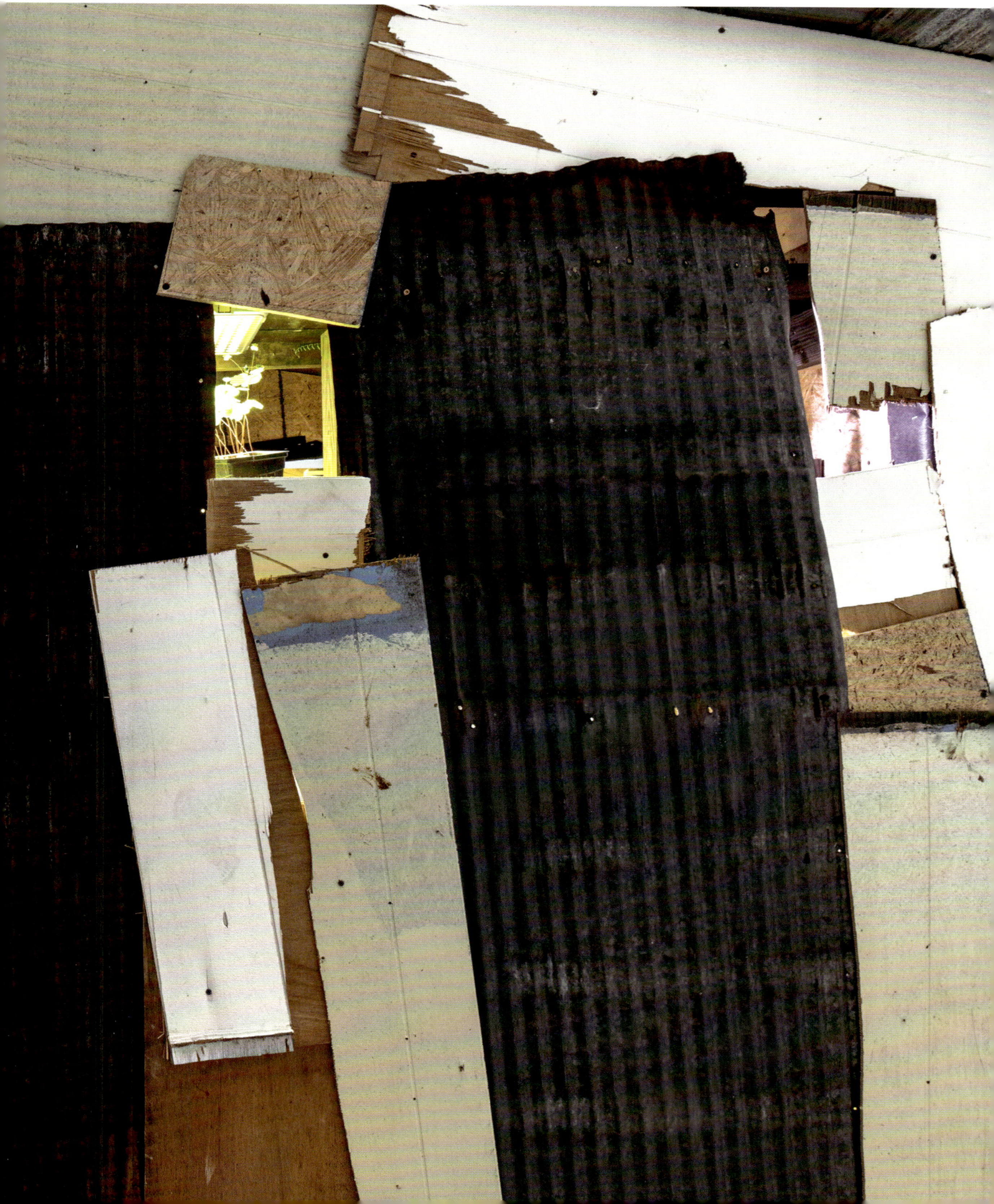

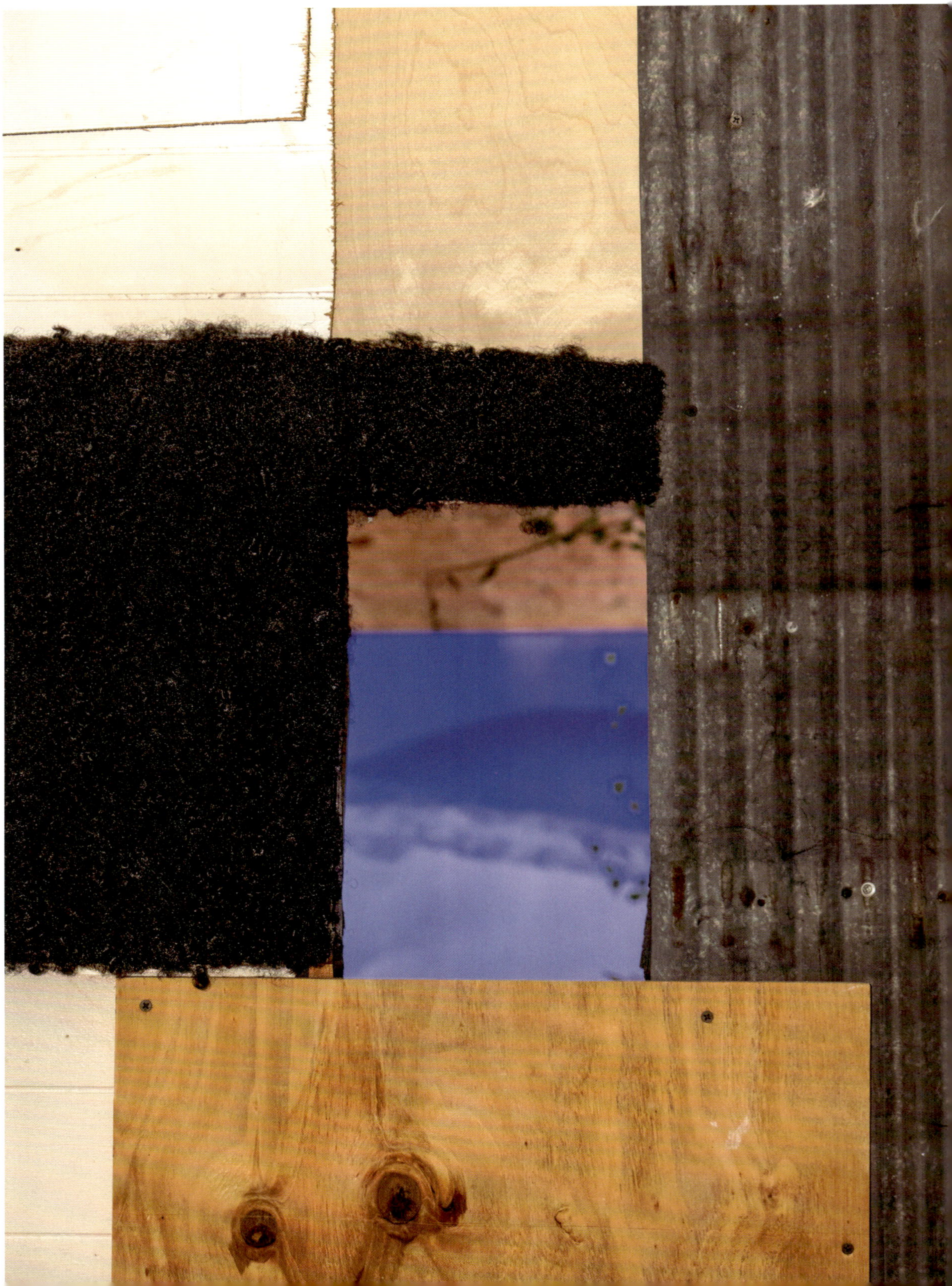

The Distraction of Symbolism (detail), 2019. Courtesy of the artist.

birthing from the bottom

DANIELLE M. PURIFOY

On the bottom of the barrel what Katherine McKittrick calls a more "humanly workable" definition of life is being created.
— ALEXIS PAULINE GUMBS, "This Instant: June Jordan and a Black Feminist Poetics of Architecture"

Can we deliver a black world to our future? An abundant arrival, a breathing black loam birth?

Let's start at the Bottom.

The Bottom is a landscape, an ecosystem, a social positioning.

It is a global black space that minds no colonial boundary, no nation's gate. It connects its people through their common stories and experiences. The Bottom is connected through its intimate knowledge of simultaneous terror and joy, violent extraction and cultural production, danger and safety, poison and healing. The Bottom is a land that refuses to be wasted. It finds a way to conserve. It makes a way out of no way.

The Bottom, in the black feminist tradition, in the work of way-makers such as June Jordan and Alexis Pauline Gumbs and Katherine McKittrick, is the space where possibility exists for true revolutionary loving liberation—the end of colonialism and massacre and marginality. The end of disposability, through the necessary practice of indispensability, rejecting individualism in favor of the collective, through shared economies, through communal networks of care, through tending the Earth as a life force, rather than a fungible commodity.

The Bottom is the entanglement of black peoples with the extraction and commodification of natures for the development of wealth and power—for the sustaining of white-dominated political space. According to Charles Mills, a Jamaican-American political philosopher, the black peoples and spaces constituting the Bottom are [mis]construed as the morally debased and waste-producing parts of the body politic—in other words, as a wilderness to be acted upon by "civilized" white space (Mills 2001). Black people under this white imaginary are thus part of an undifferentiated extractable resource. As Jamaican economist George Beckford notes, this is the character of the continuing plantation economy—the replication of colonialism and its ecology onto contemporary landscapes, through new configurations of resource extraction and wealth production (Beckford 1999). These include:

—the voracious wrenching of fossil fuels from rainforest ecosystems that supply much of the world's oxygen, and the massacre and expulsion of peoples living there

—the mass confined breeding of hogs and poultry for global meat consumption and their lagoons of feces and aborted fetuses, which leak contaminants into the air and drinking water of neighboring black and brown and poor communities

—the chronic flows of raw sewage in places from rural North Carolina to downtown Kingston

—the systemic and violent displacement of small farmers by multinational agribusinesses through global monoculture practices that render lands barren

—the patenting of life itself, through the denial of reproductive rights

—the denial, against overwhelming evidence, of a changing climate, while casting away those displaced by rising waters, extinct species, and desertified lands

— the consolidation and isolation of power and wealth so far from the sites of production that their holders believe they can survive without the Bottom—indeed, without a functioning planet

— the conditions generated by these configurations demonstrate that this system cannot continue. When it crumbles, what will emerge?

The constitutive subordination and "thingification" of black peoples and non-human species requires a black feminist articulation of liberation, which itself requires a major change in the current characterization and valuation of our ecosystems. To deliver a black world to our future is to alter our relationship to both humanity and the ecologies that make humans possible. It requires no less than the reconstitution of what we think of as a planet, an ecosystem, a society.

Central to the work of that transformation is the imaginary, the speculative "what if" or "what could be." In their brilliant edited collection of stories on social movements, Adrienne Maree Brown and Walidah Imarisha define the process of social change: "Whenever we try to envision a world without war, without violence, without prisons, without capitalism, we are engaging in speculative fiction" (Brown and Imarisha 2015).

Invoking the groundbreaking and prescient work of black speculative fiction author Octavia Butler, whose novels were deeply concerned with the collapse of racial capitalism and the possibilities of creating ecologically sound and "humanly workable" worlds for black peoples, Brown and Imarisha argue that stretching beyond the realm of the real, crossing into spaces of perceived impossibility, is the only way that marginalized peoples have ever survived and made a way for themselves. Speculative fiction is thus about staking claim to a future and making the birth of that future possible and ultimately inevitable.

The Bottom is the center of such visionary fiction; it is already where impossibilities are made real because it is the space least served by the extant system. It invents as a means of survival; it imagines a version of the world where its people breathe and move their bodies fearlessly, dwell wherever they land, sit on porches in peace, drink clean water, grow food in their own backyards, and reproduce new lives that thrive however they come.

Such impossibilities are worked on in the everydayness of making full, rich, human black lives. The gestures need not all be grand to create this alternative world. Worlds can be altered by simple acts such as planting gardens, composting food, and building relationships. It is not simply that these acts alone are revolutionary or liberatory—though they may well be. It is that collectively they make conditions possible that did not exist before. They make the work of change more transparent and viable; they make the present system seem less inevitable.

The investment in interrupting plantation economies, in telling new visionary stories, is a central concern of Deborah Anzinger's creative practice. Like Imarisha and Brown and Butler, Anzinger recognizes the progression from simple actions to speculative social change, which in her work are inextricable from ecological transformation and healing.

The observations in *An Unlikely Birth* demonstrate the myriad ways in which the toxic slow death delivered to the Bottom—often under the guise of sustaining human livelihoods for those in power—is entangled with the insistent lives of people and non-human beings. The metabolic reproduction of poison in growing living bodies, politically construed as resilience, perpetuates an environmental "riskscape" where toxins create cellular imprints that are passed through generations, compounded by other forms of trauma—from state violence to hunger to deforestation to flooding (Morello-Frosch 2011).

Anzinger's assemblages of organic and inorganic matter—hair, living botanicals, and petroleum-based plastics—insist on the collapse of separate categories of "human" and "nature" for no less than the sake of our survival. The embeddedness of the synthetic, the toxic, which we have now globally absorbed at the cellular level, is both a statement of our current crisis and a visionary demand that we grow out of it.

As part of this ultimatum, Anzinger directs us to the conditions of reproduction, which is, ultimately, where our sovereignty must be gained. How can the Bottom, where mothering is most precarious, vilified, and devalued, birth and support conditions that make life possible again? How can the life birthed by the Bottom comprise a seamless collective of beings existing in interconnected lifecycles?

One proposed way to achieve this seeming impossibility is through the legal animism of non-anthropogenic life—that is, the assignation of rights to the flora, fauna, soils, waterways, and microorganisms that comprise Earth's ecosystem (Biemann and Tavares 2014; Demos 2016). Giving legal standing to life that cannot speak for itself in human-centered space is the way we currently know how to protect that life within an anthropocentric world. Yet laws are politicized to serve humans in power; rights are rooted in individualism, and are routinely stripped or abandoned to subordinate humans who can and do speak for themselves.

These are practical steps for the current world; they can be useful because they can make us begin to expand the definition of "us" to mean all living things. But more importantly, they may even help us to discover, finally, that our systems of justice have no relationship to truth, equity, or fairness, and that our relations are (and must be) much bigger than a set of social contracts and individual rights.

What would it mean to mother a black world for our future, from the Bottom? This speculative fiction is perhaps the most important story for us to discover; its possibilities are limitless. We could imagine—in the midst of apocalyptic conditions, with walls erected to enforce every border, with basic resources rendered inaccessible to all but a very few cowardly humans, with drowned cities and desperate and risky migrations, with species collapse and famine and aquatic dead zones—that we might find multiple spaces long considered dead and discarded quietly, almost imperceptibly, tending and nurturing and incubating something so strange and tender as to be unrecognizable to this world.

REFERENCES

Beckford, George L. 1991. *Persistent Poverty: Underdevelopment in Plantation Economies of the Third World.* Kingston, Jamaica: University of West Indies Press.

Biemann, Ursula, and Paulo Tavares. 2014. Forest Law—*Selva Juridica*. Exhibition catalog. East Lansing: Eli and Edythe Broad Art Museum, Michigan State University.

Brown, Adrienne Maree, and Walidah Imarisha, eds. 2015. *Octavia'sBrood: Science Fiction Stories from Social Justice Movements.* Chico, CA: AK Press.

Demos, T. J. 2016. *Decolonizing Nature: Contemporary Art and the Politics of Ecology.* Berlin: Sternberg.

Gumbs, Alexis Pauline. 2013. "This Instant: June Jordan and a Black Feminist Poetics of Architecture," Online posting, 22 July 2013. www.scribd.com doc/155271148/ This-Instant-June-Jordan-and-a-Black-Feminist-Poetics-of-Architecture.

Mills, Charles W. 2001. "Black Trash." In *Faces of Environmental Racism*, edited by Laura Westra and Bill E. Lawson, 79–91. Lanham, MD: Rowman & Littlefield.

Morello-Frosch, Rachel, et al. 2011. "Understanding the Cumulative Impacts of Inequalities in Environmental Health: Implications for Policy." *Health Affairs* 30, no. 5 (May): 879–87.

The Distraction of Symbolism (detail), 2019. Courtesy of the artist.

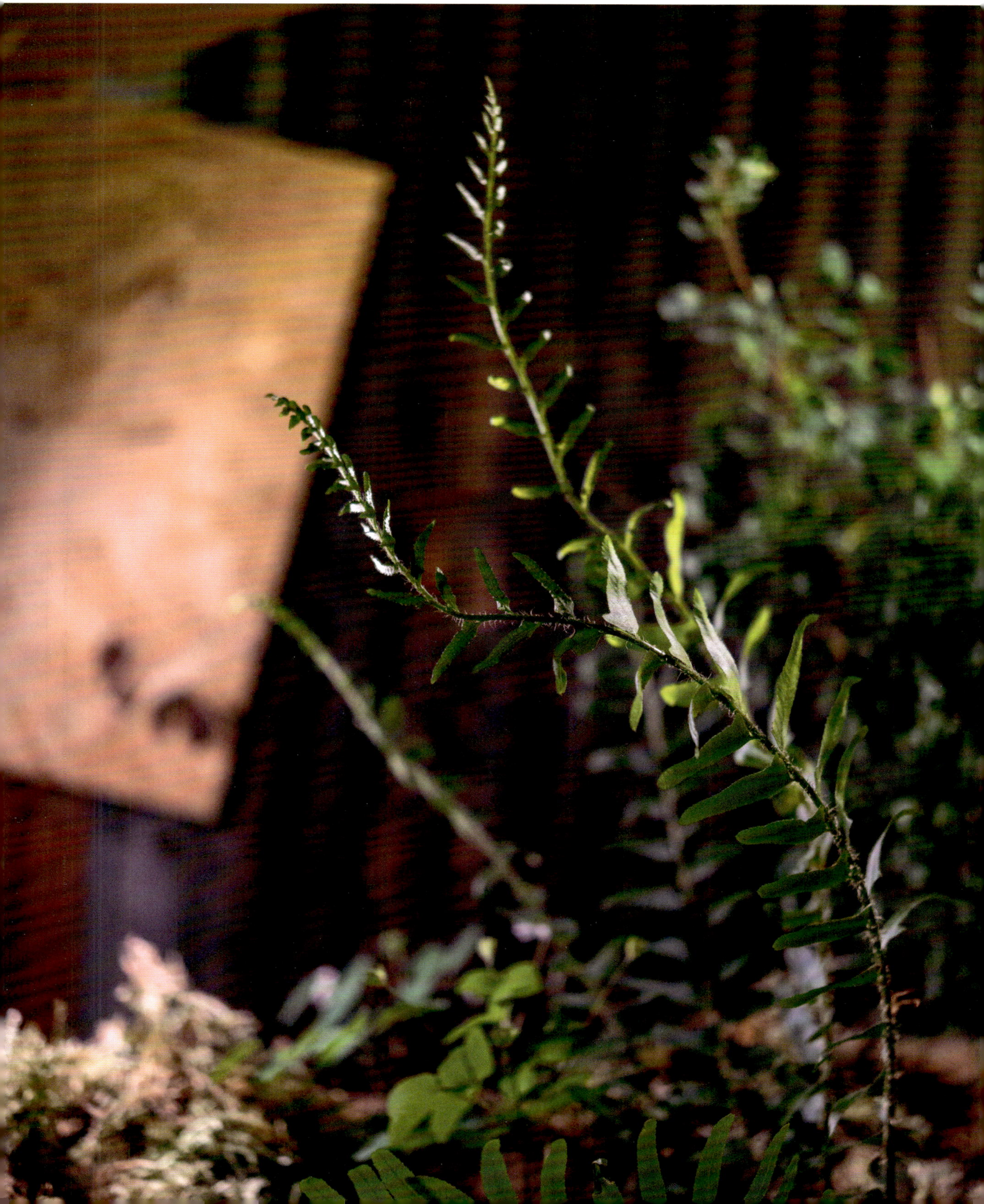

paintings and sculptures

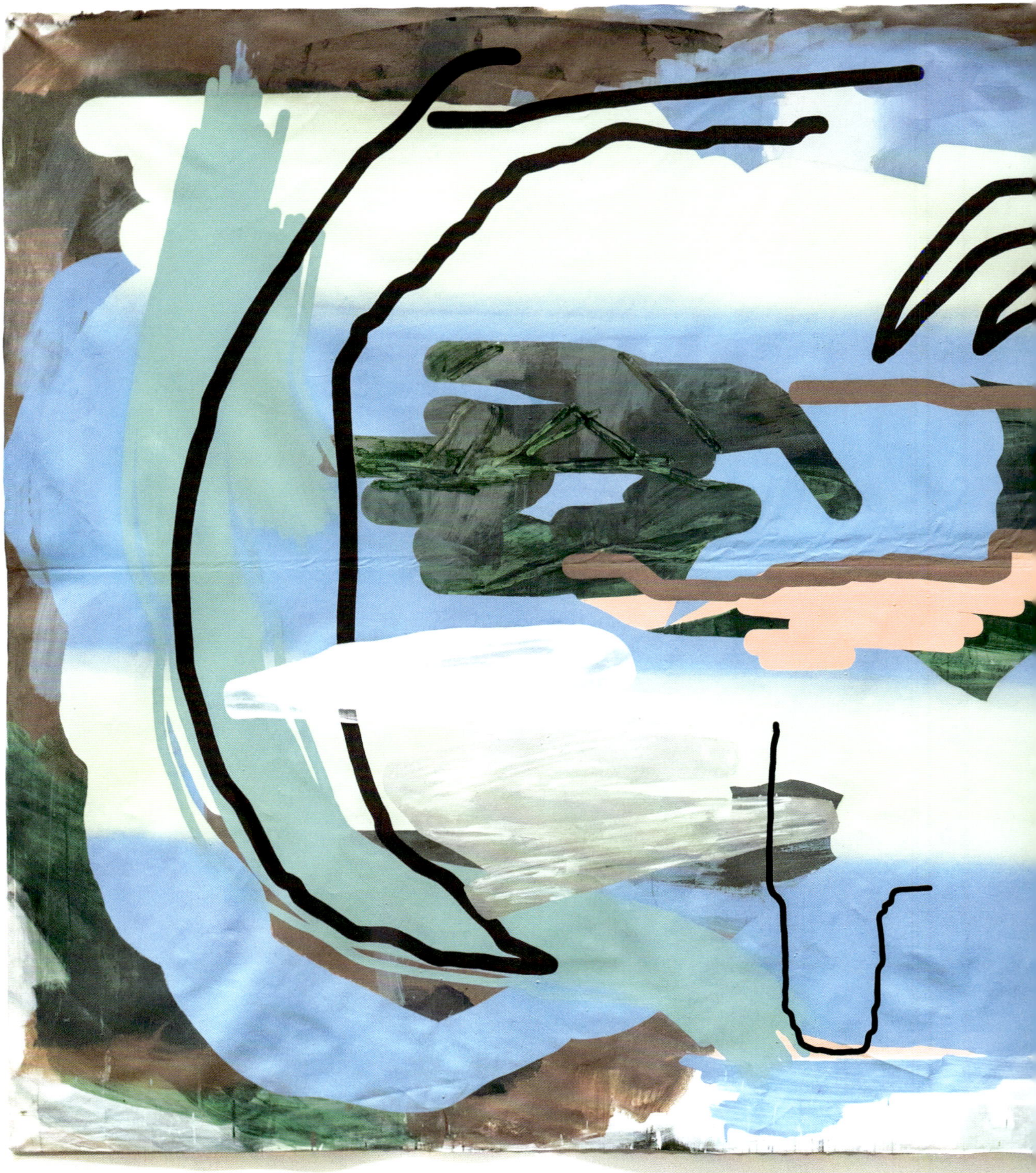

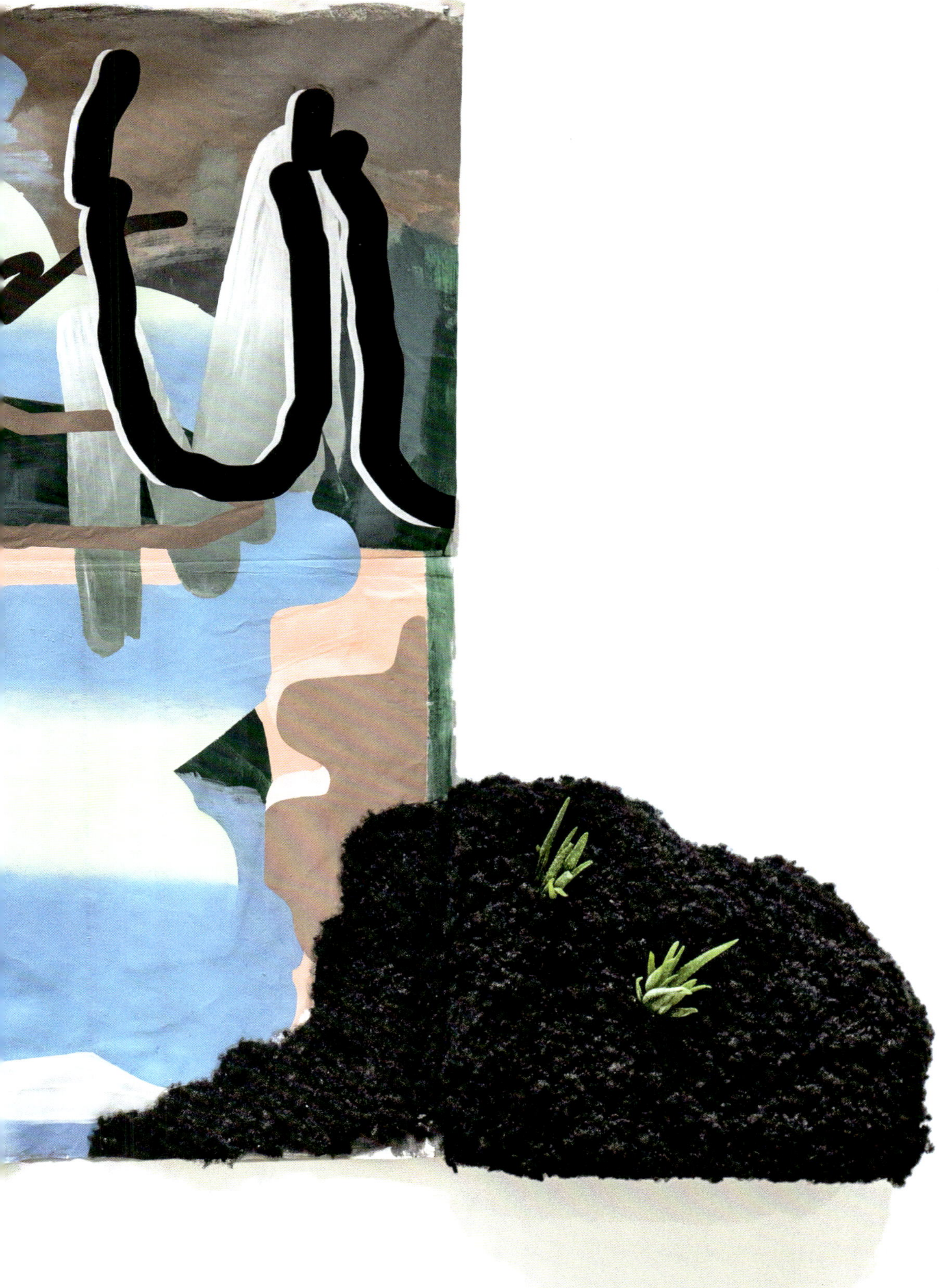

An Unlikely Birth, 2018. Courtesy of the artist.

An Unlikely Birth (detail), 2018. Courtesy of the artist.

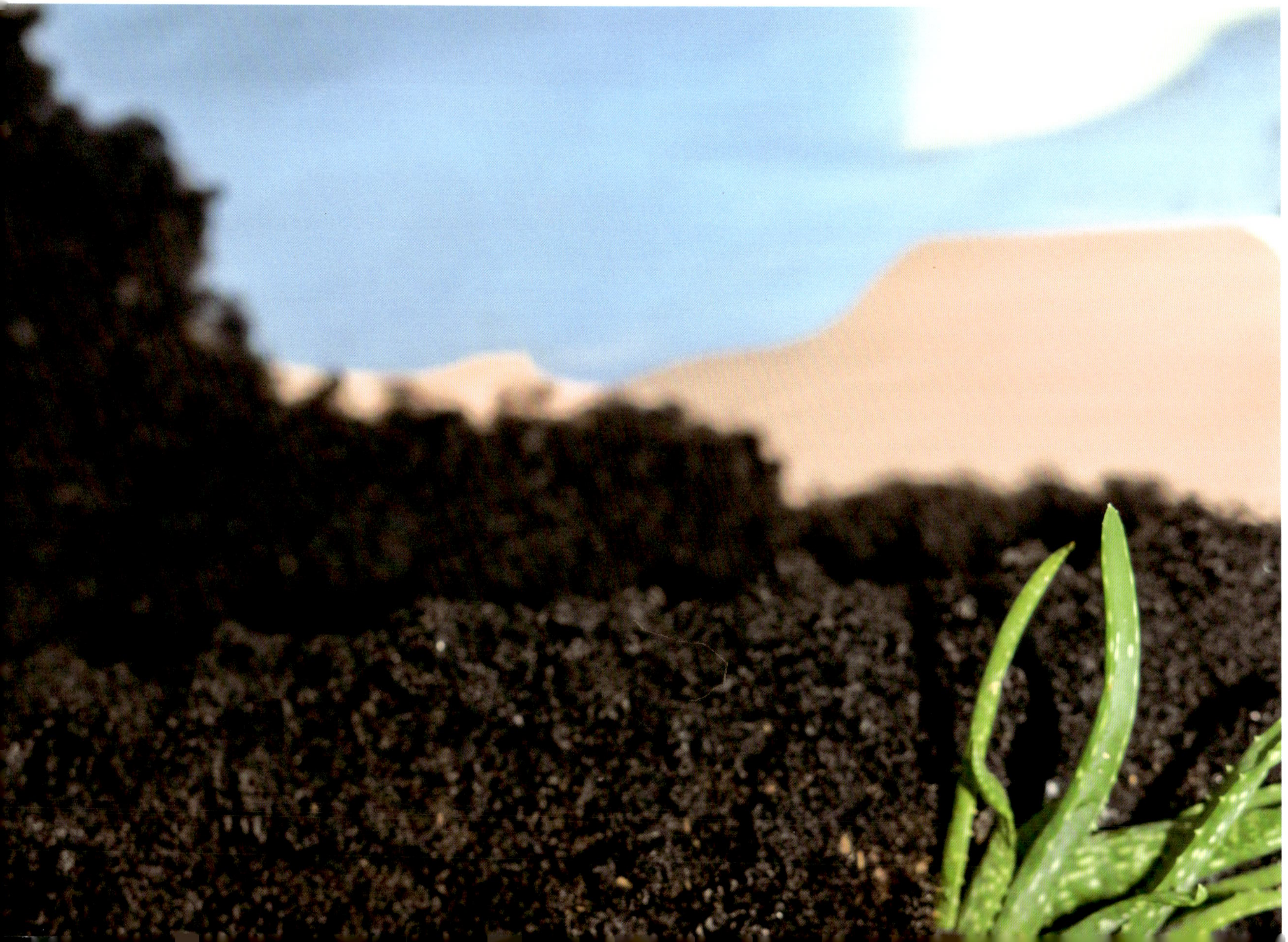

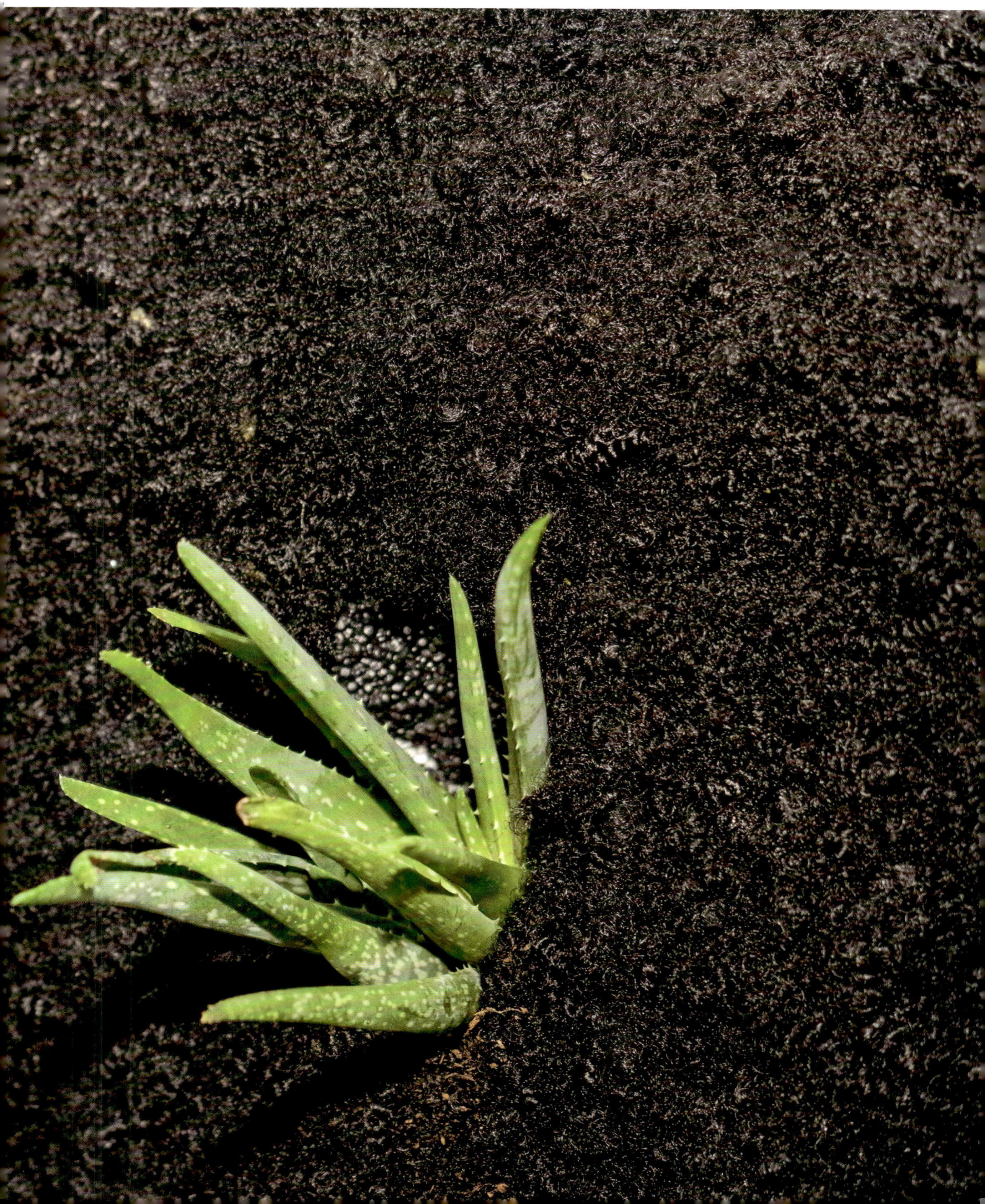

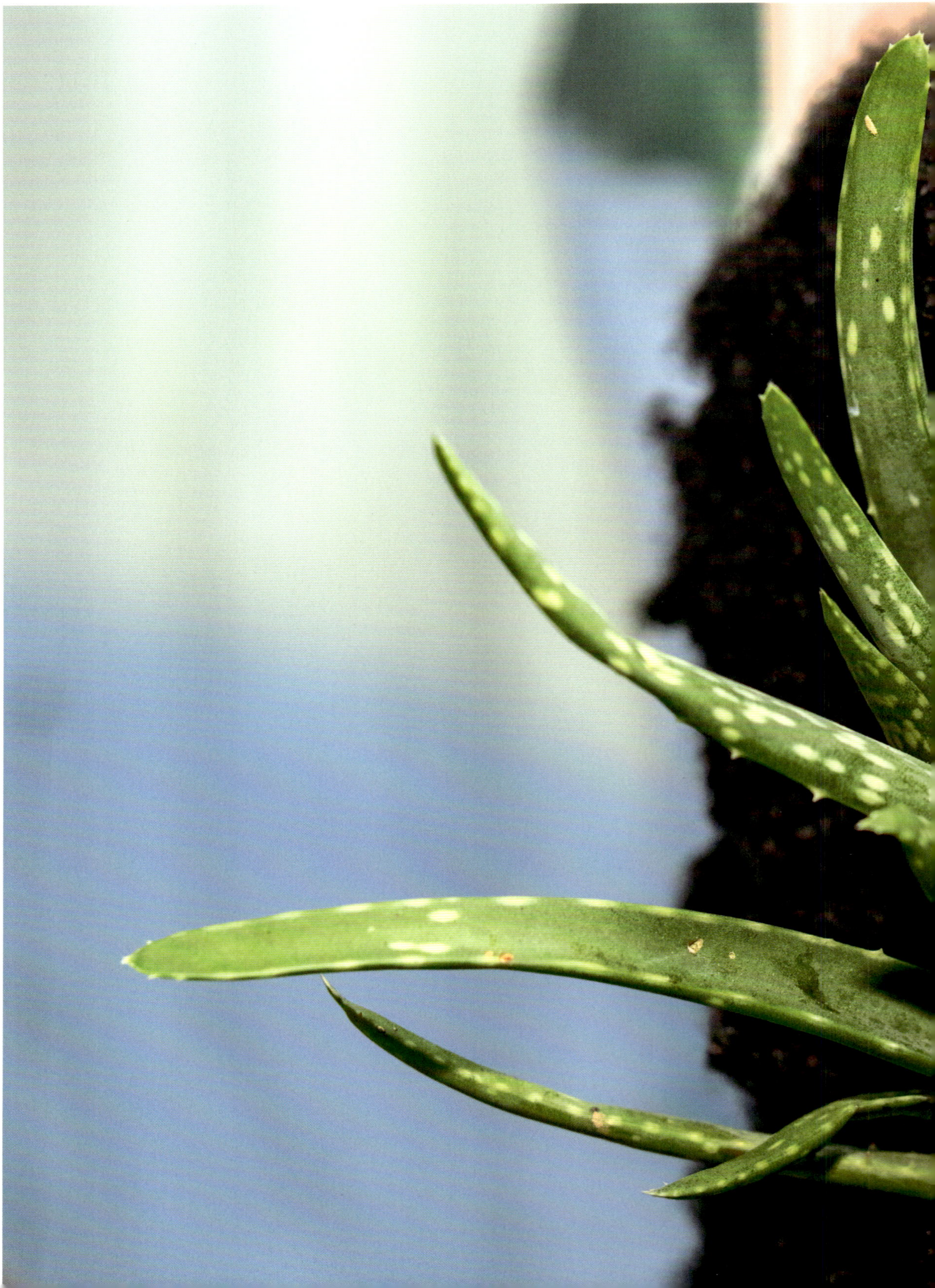

An Unlikely Birth (detail), 2018. Courtesy of the artist.

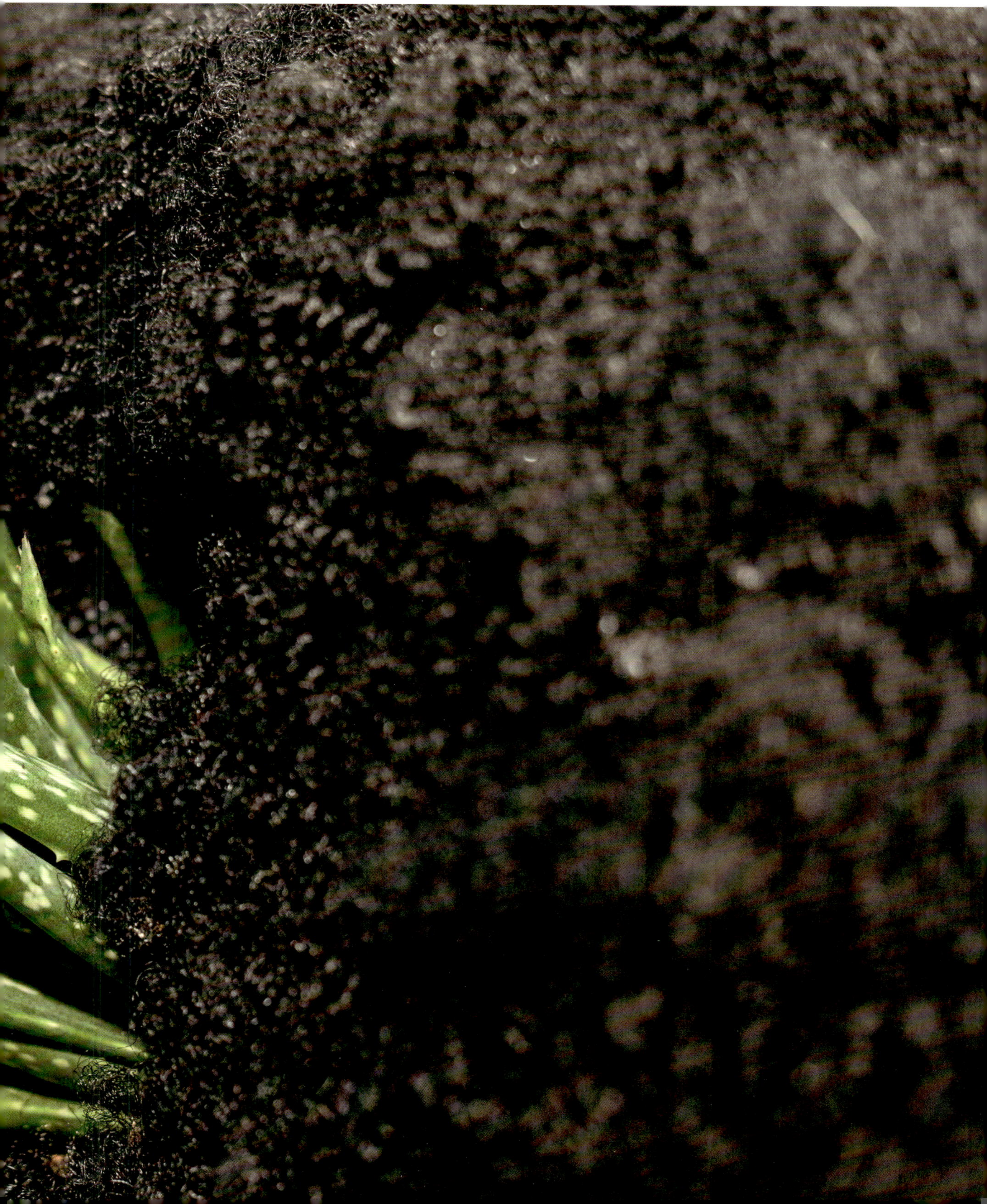

Garden, 2018. Courtesy of the artist.

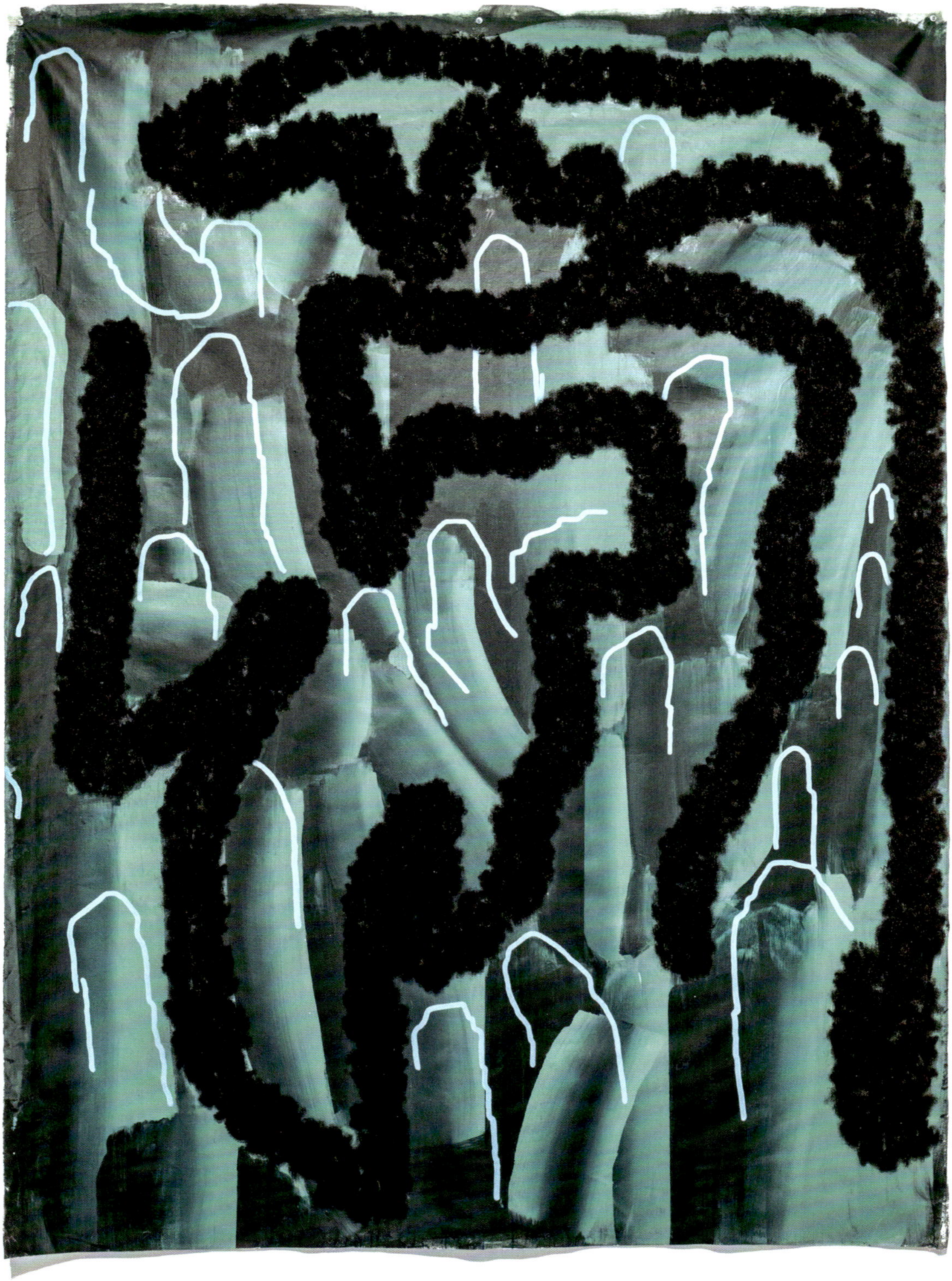

Inhospitable, 2018. Courtesy of the artist.

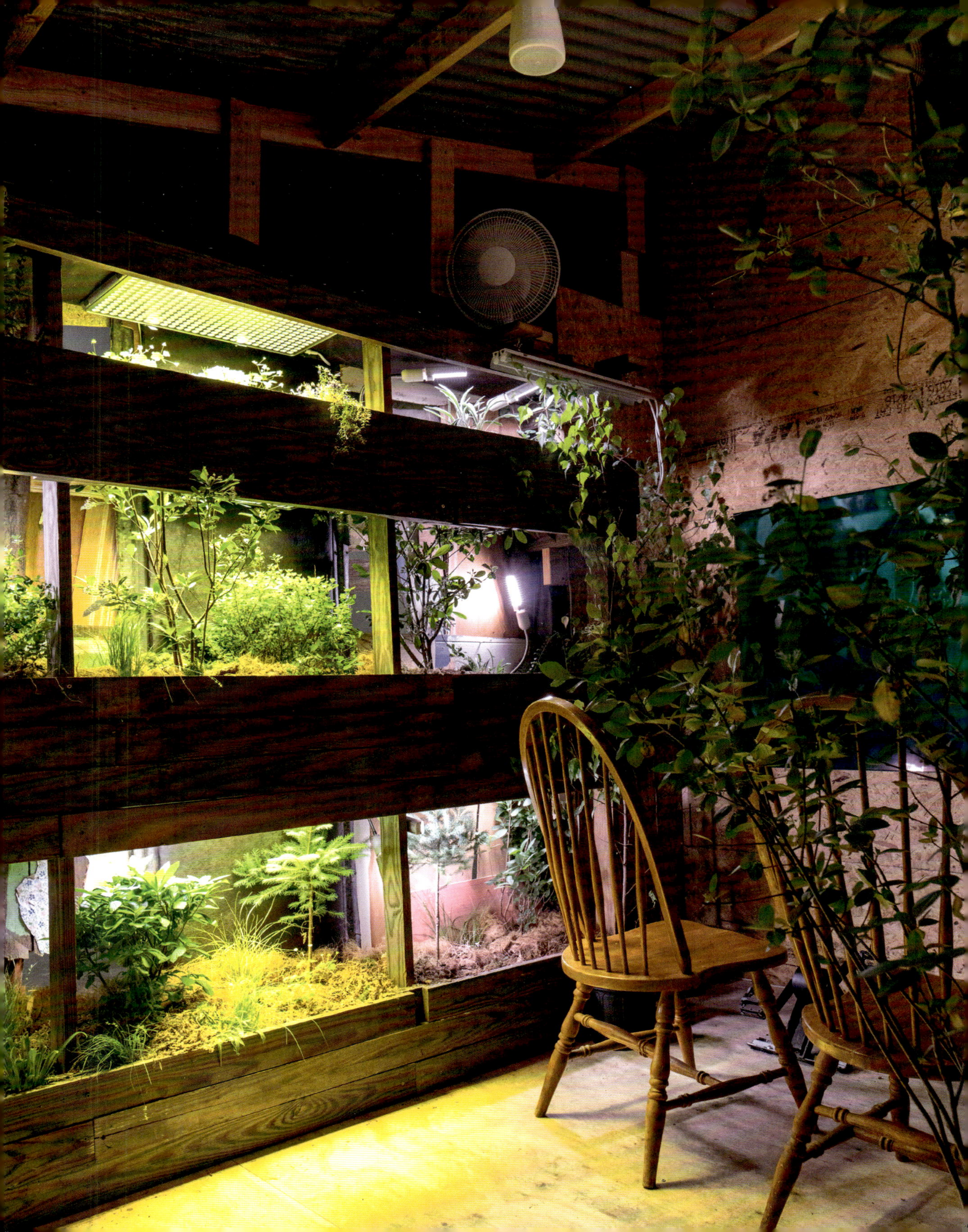

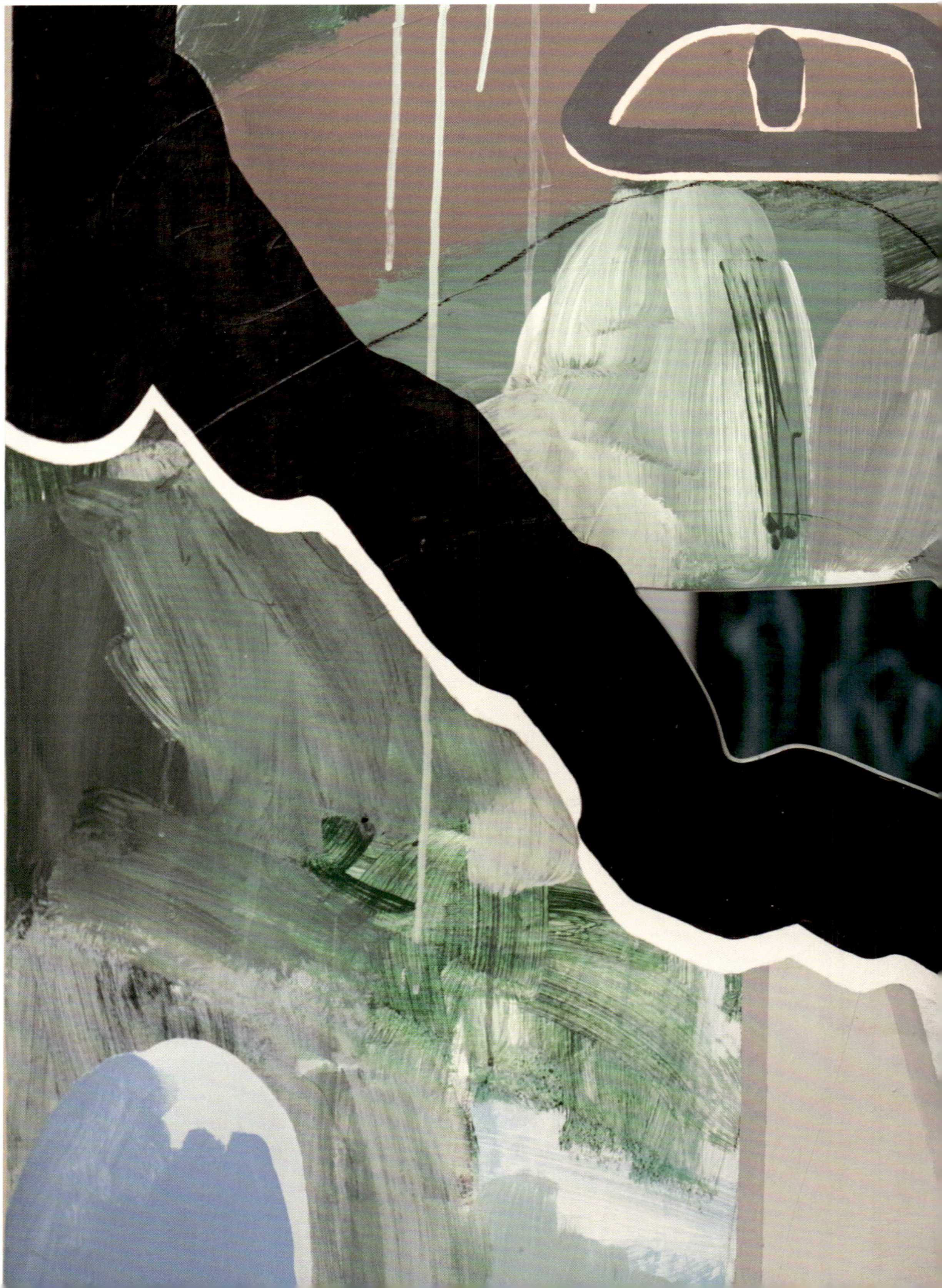

Inhospitable (detail), 2018. Courtesy of the artist.

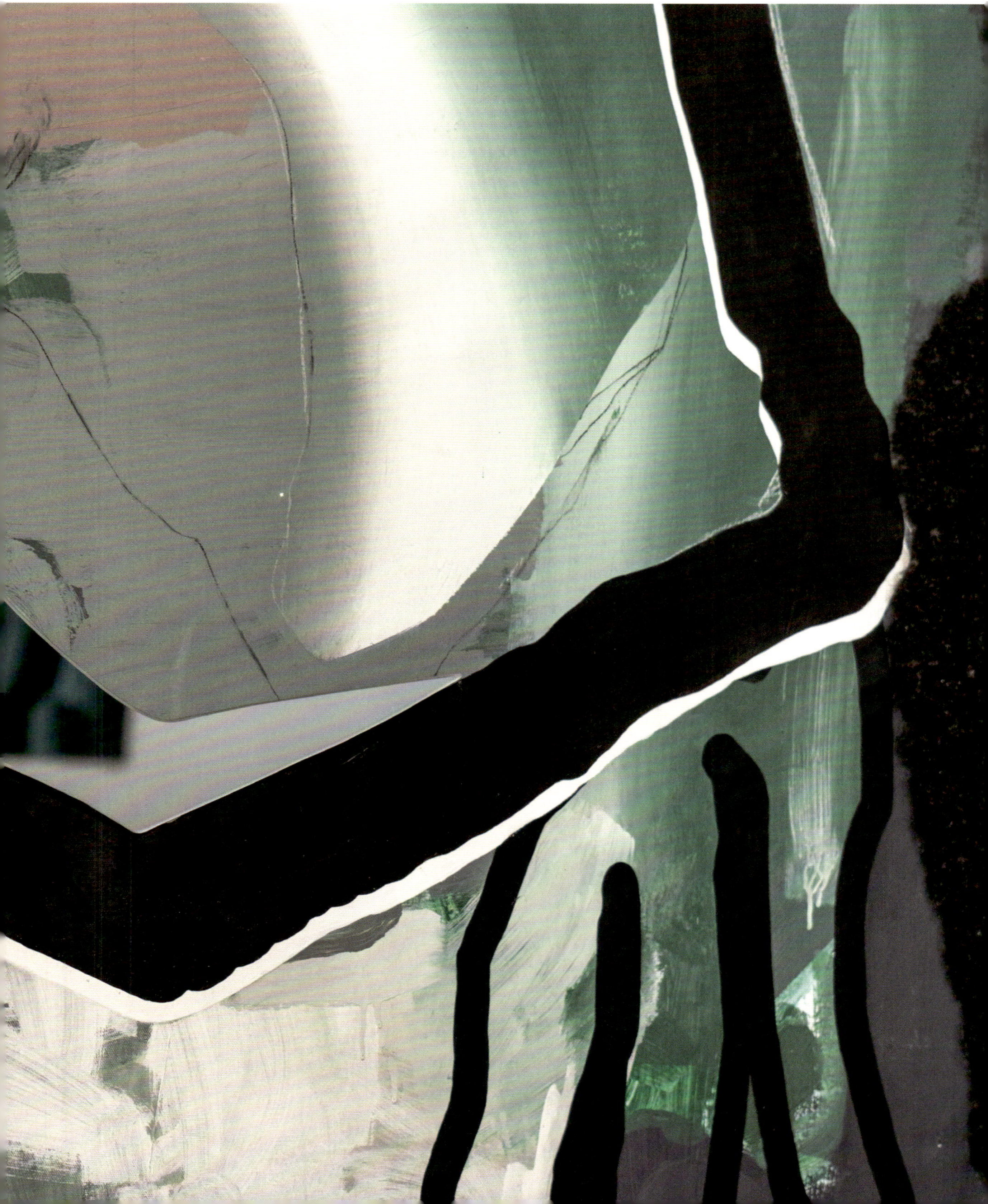

Soaked in shade, 2018. Courtesy of the artist.

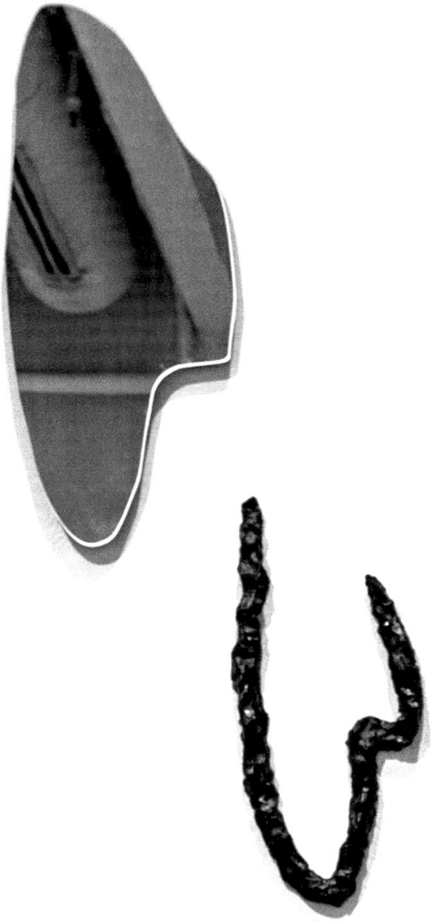

Sprout, 2019. Courtesy of the artist.

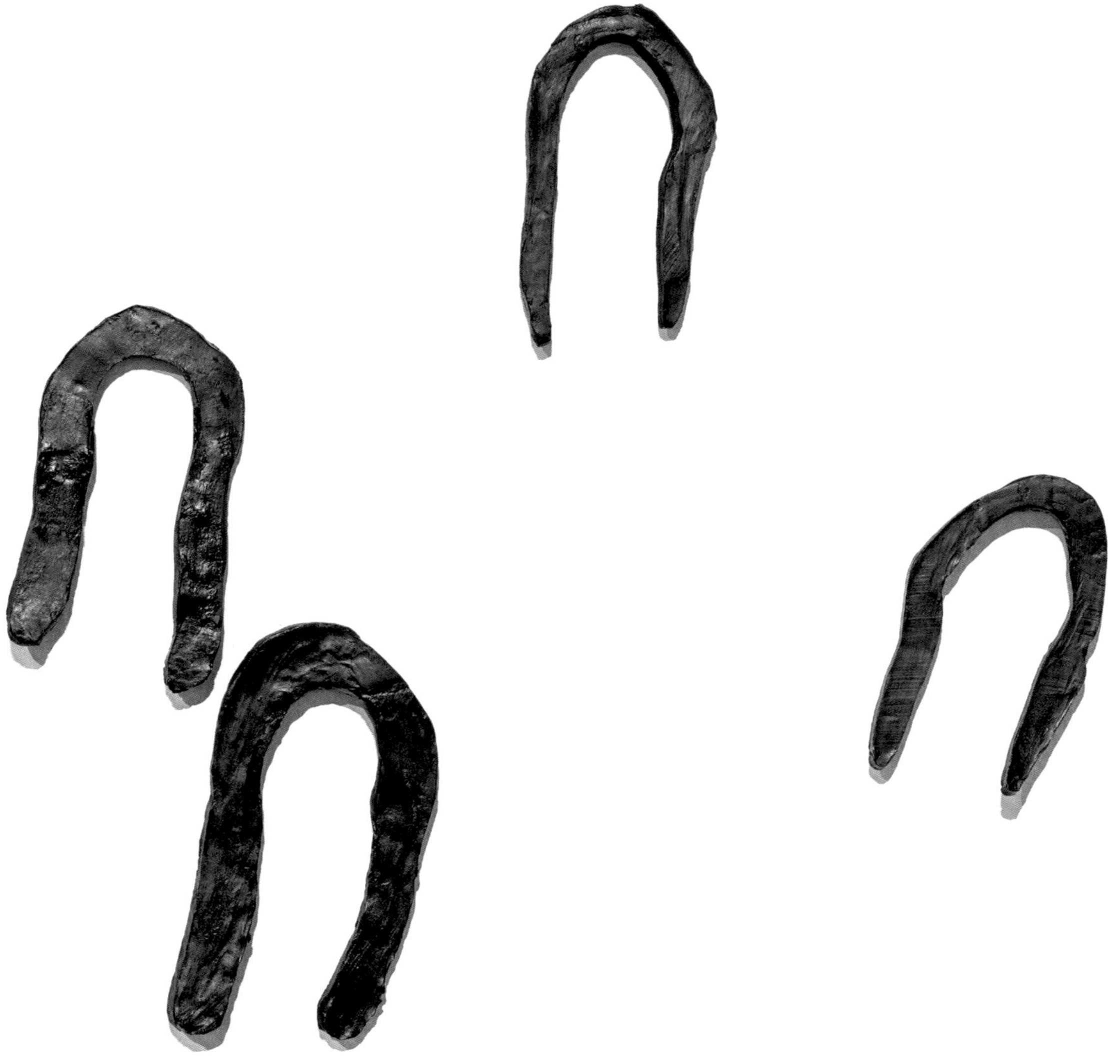

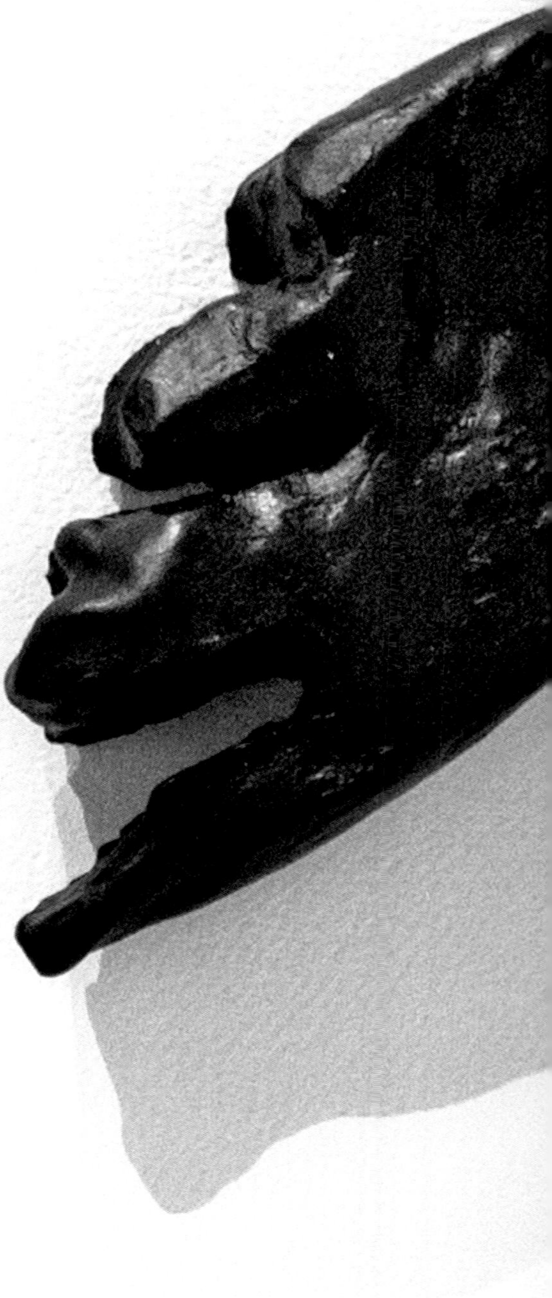

Resonant, 2017. Courtesy of the artist.

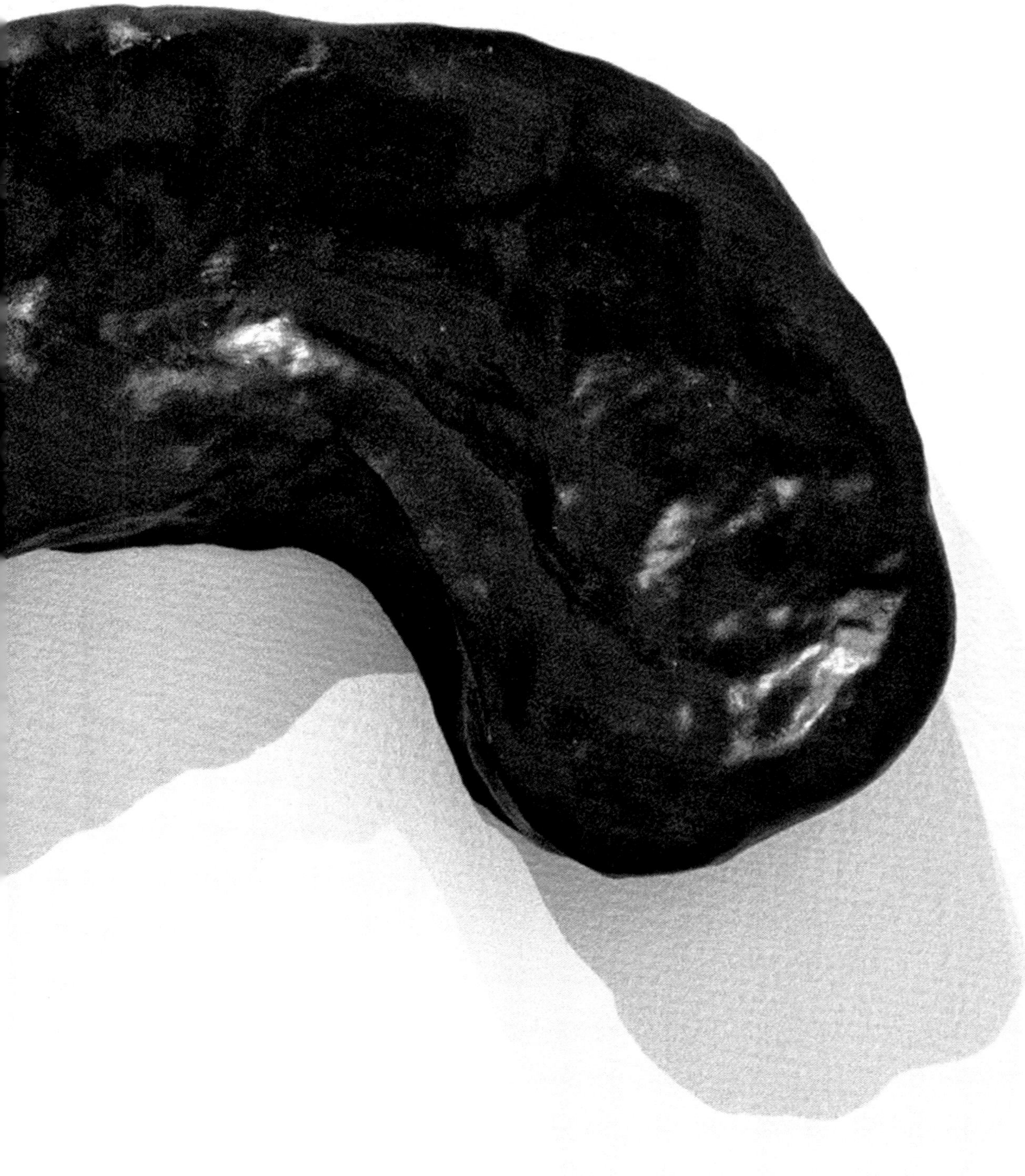

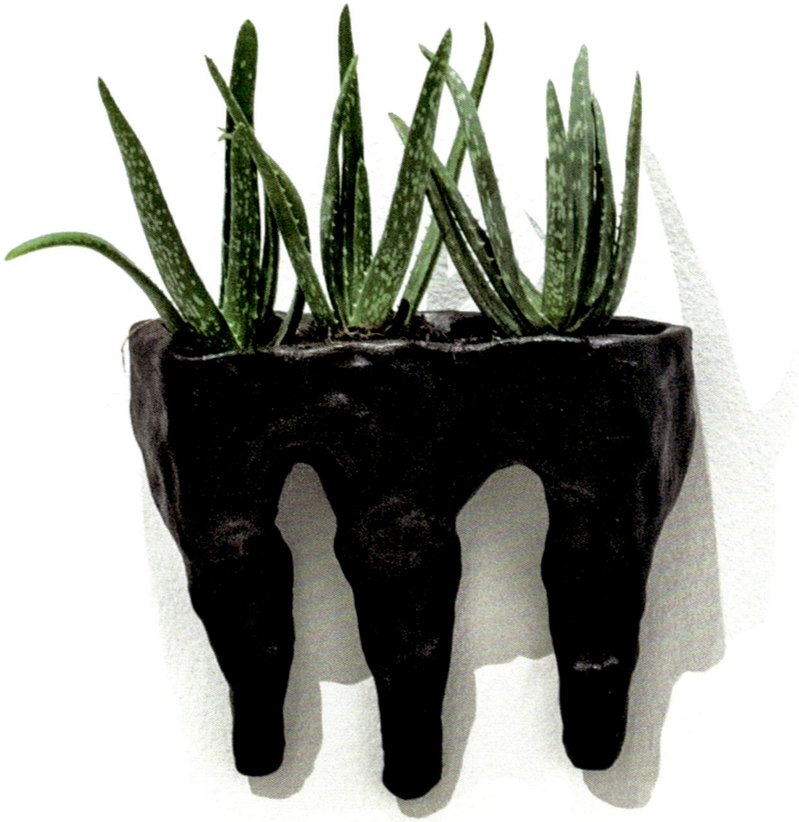

Fiction as a Vessel for Reality (left), 2016. Courtesy of the artist.

Eye #2 (right), 2019. Courtesy of the artist.

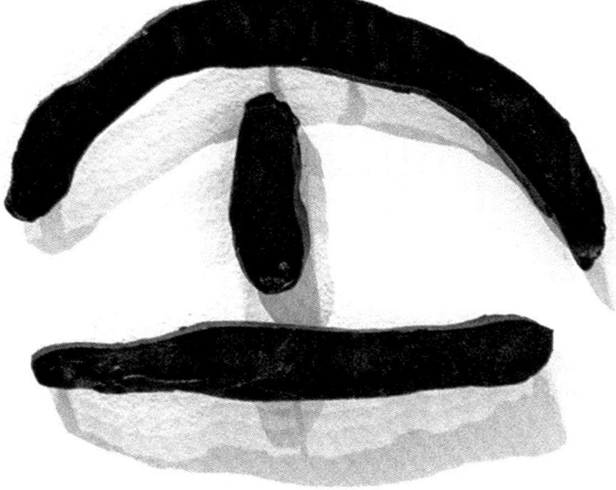

I Told You, 2016. Courtesy of the artist.

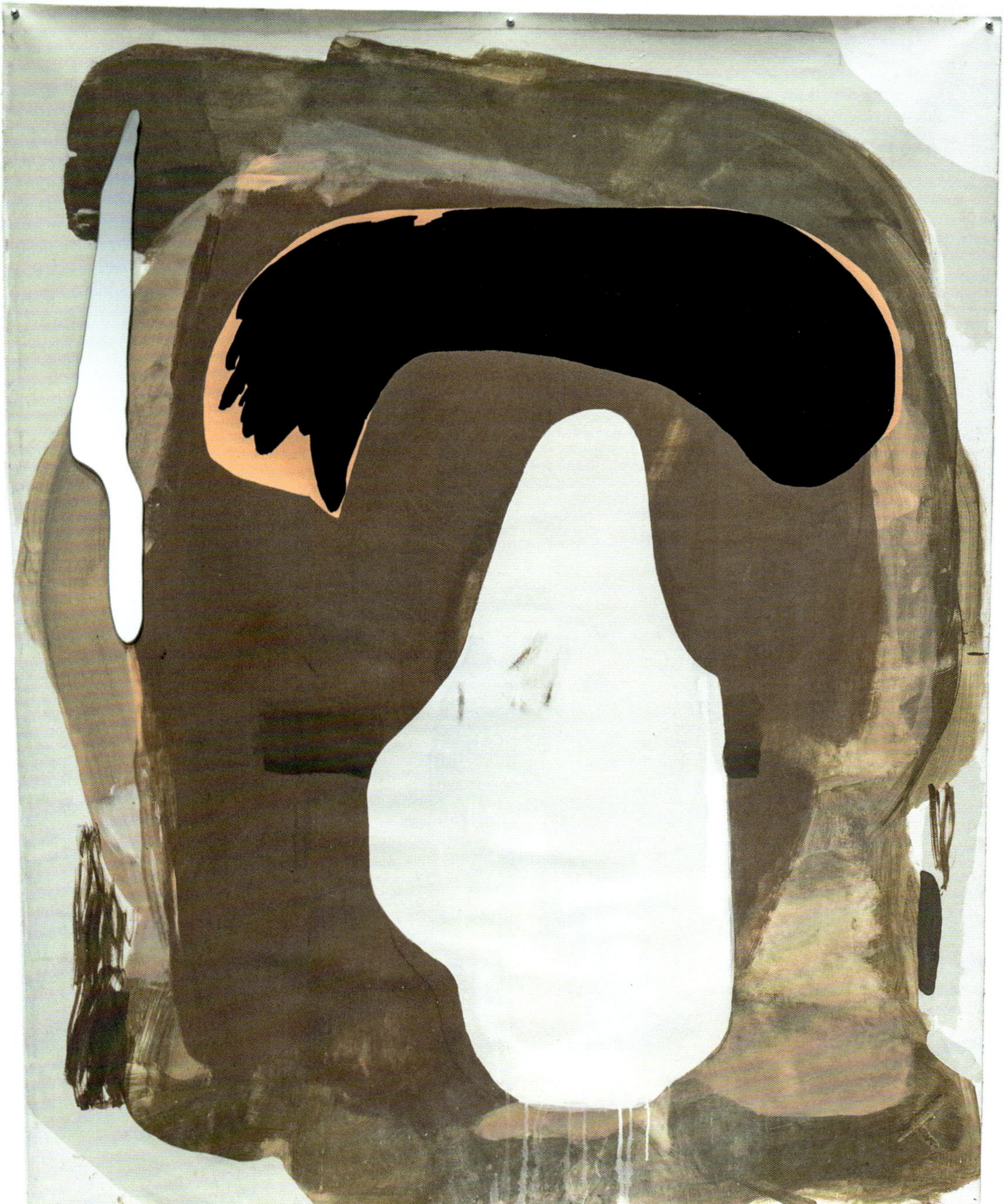

Before you realized you could be seen, I watched you soaked in the shade while I was conceiving, 2018. Courtesy of the artist.

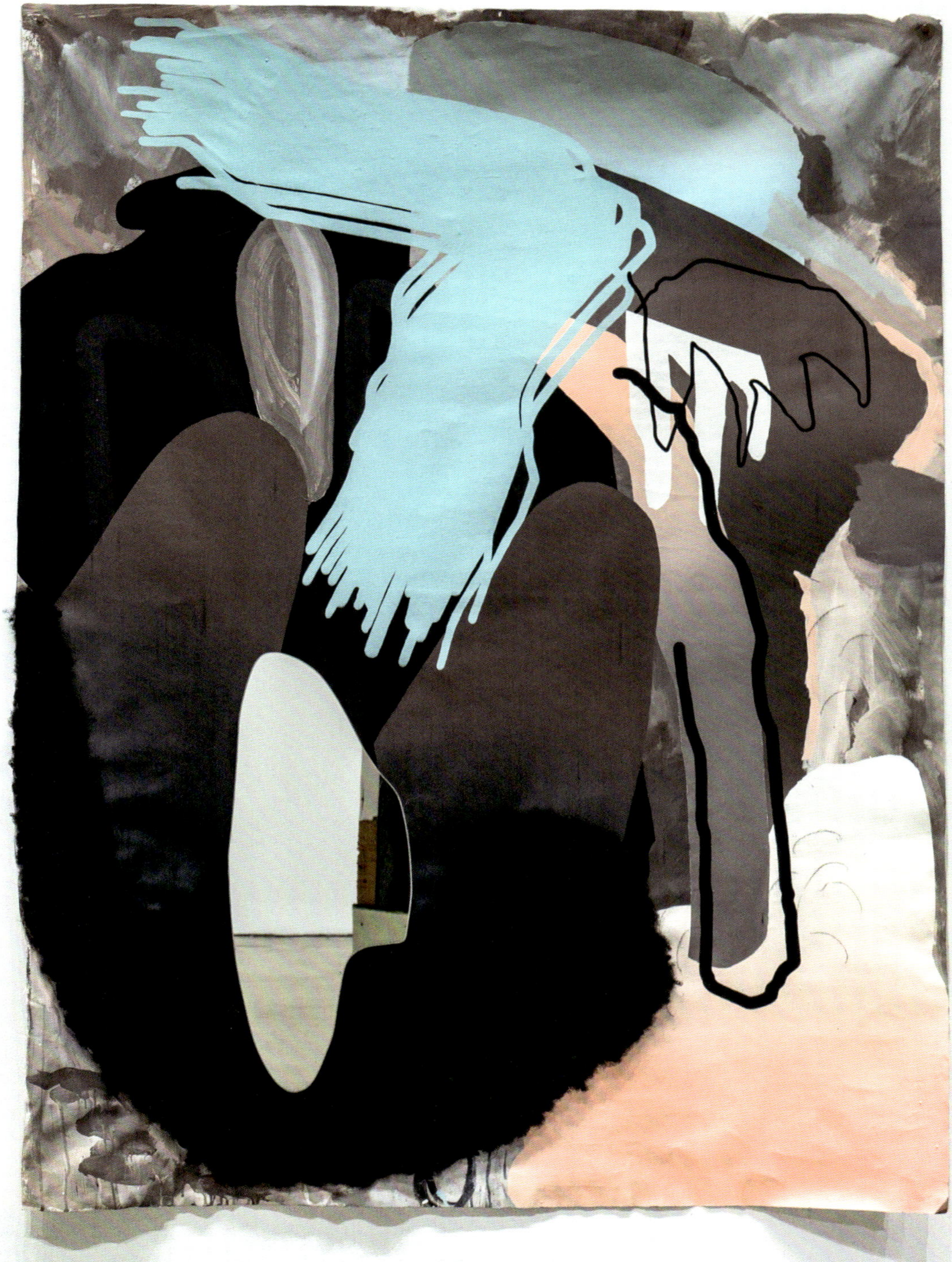

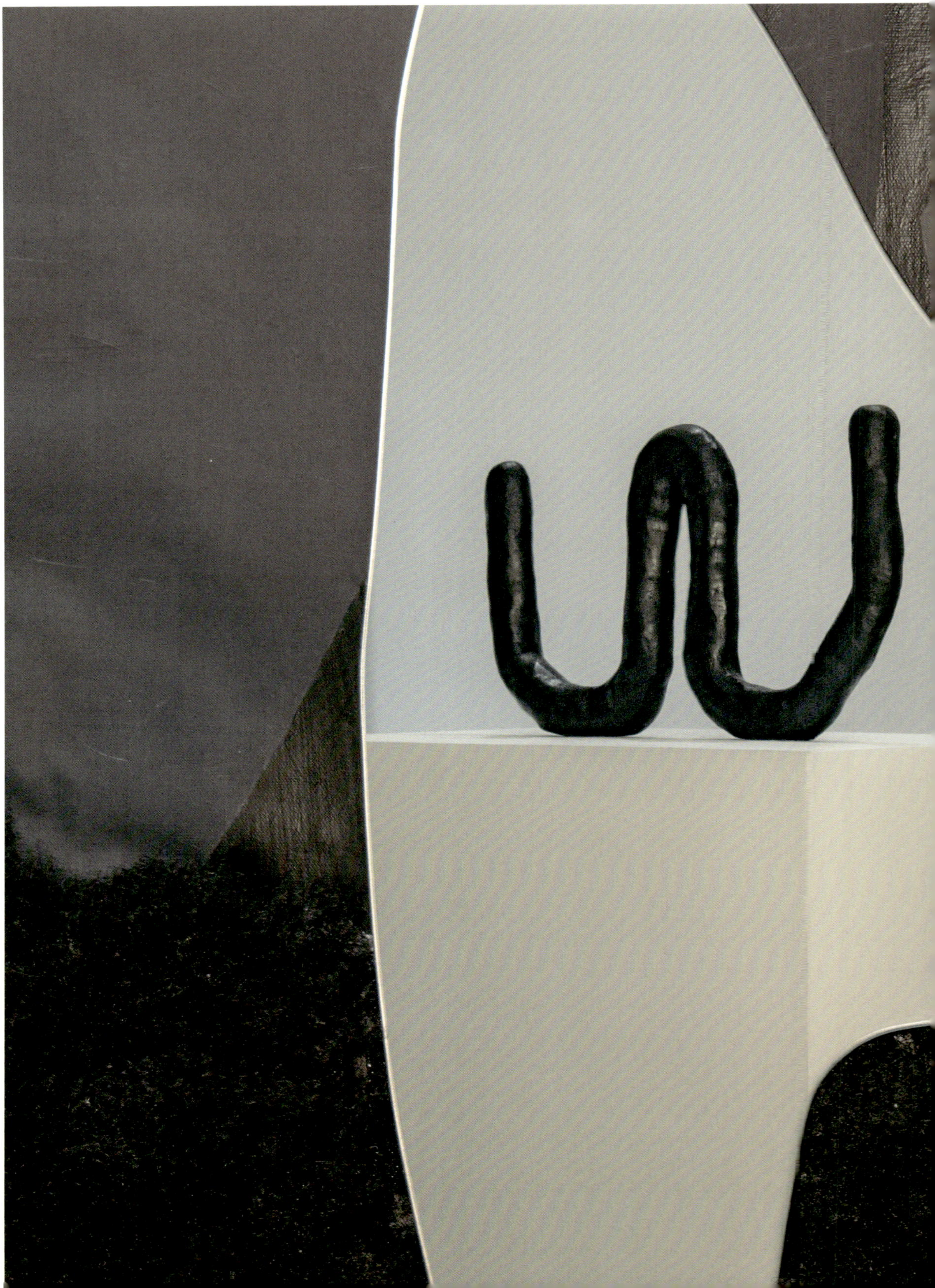

Unfeed, 2018, installation view, Deborah Anzinger: An Unlikely Birth, 2019. Institute of Contemporary Art. Courtesy of the artist.

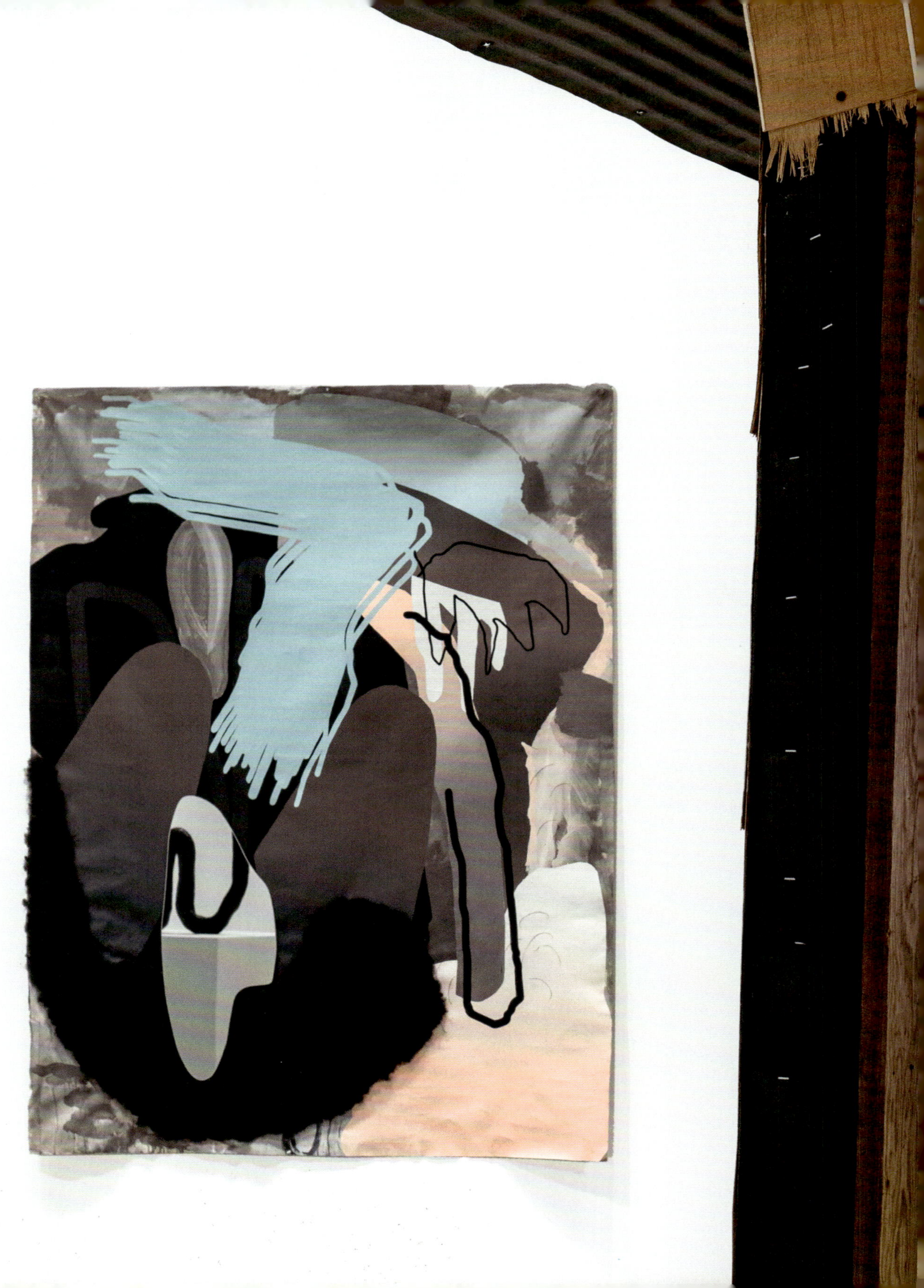

Deborah Anzinger: An Unlikely Birth, 2019, installation view, Institute of Contemporary Art, University of Pennsylvania.

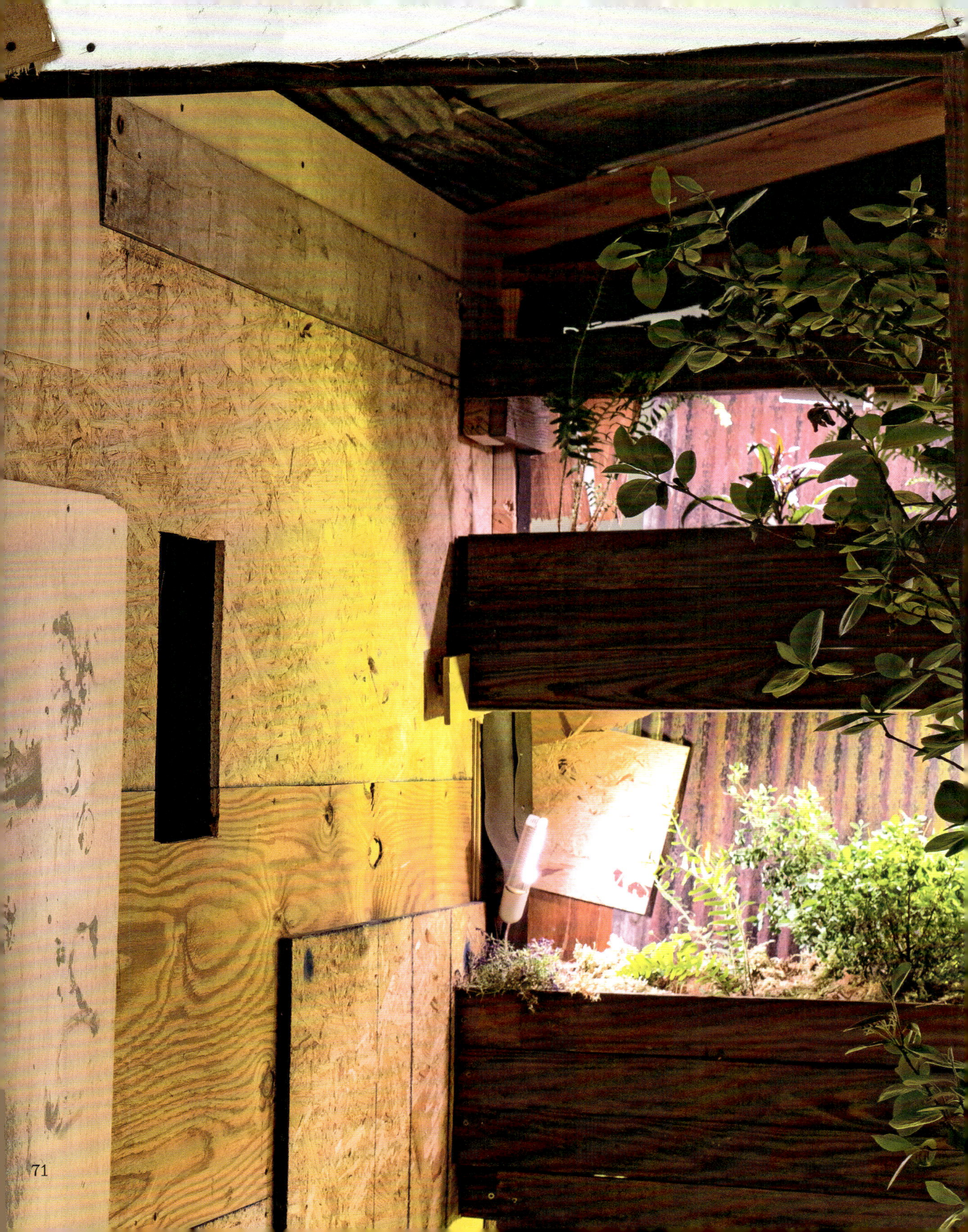

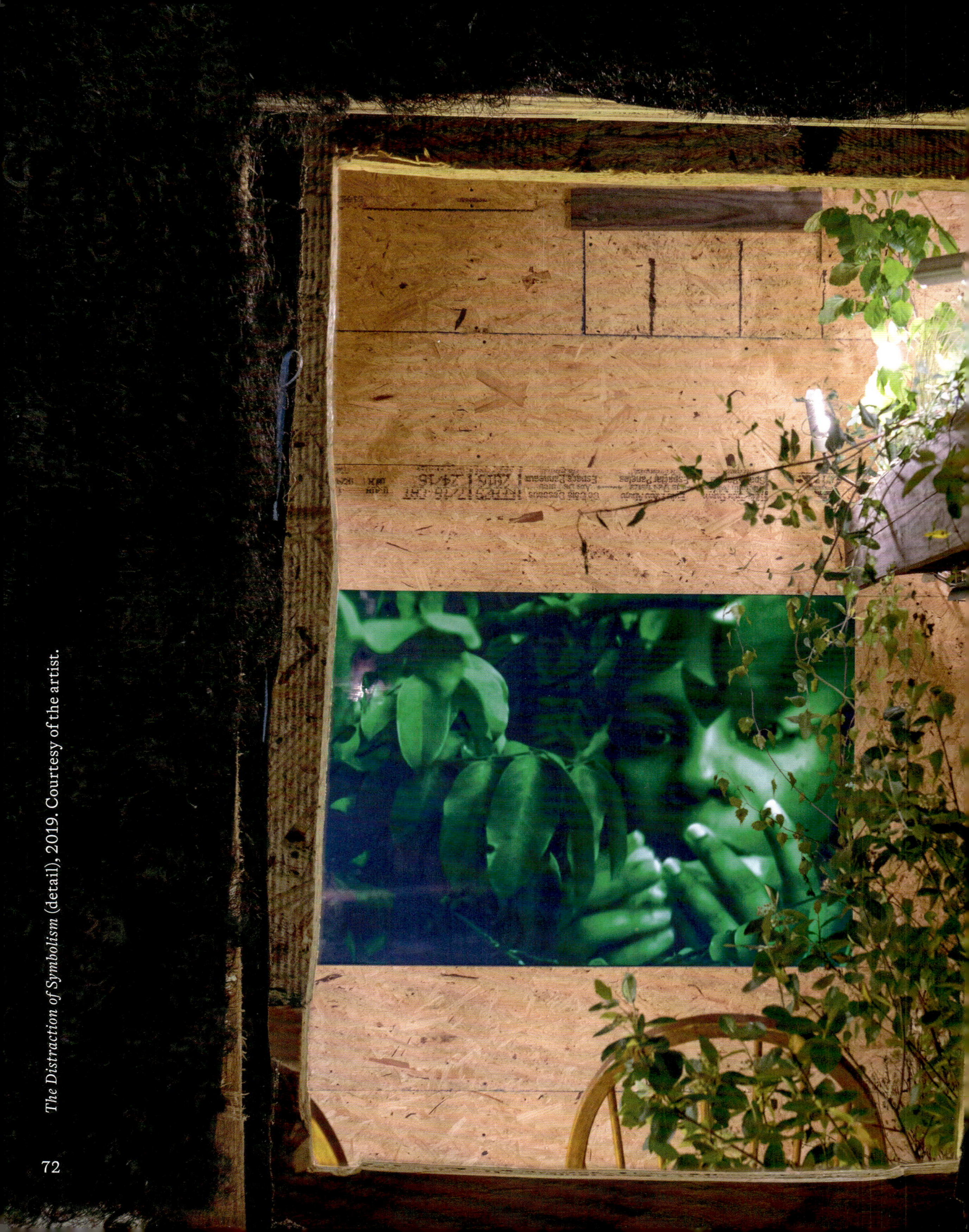

The Distraction of Symbolism (detail), 2019. Courtesy of the artist.

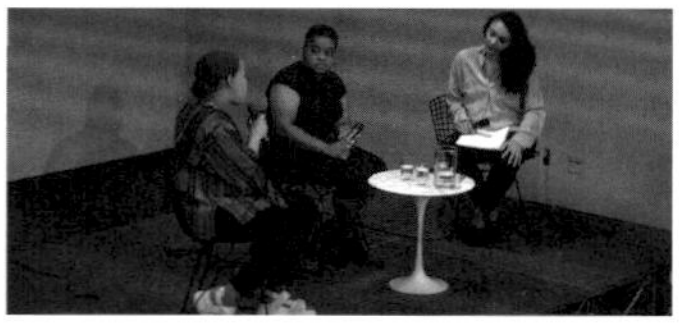

DANIELLE M. PURIFOY,
DEBORAH ANZINGER, and
DANIELLA ROSE KING during
On Hospitality public conversation.
Institute of Contemporary Art
University of Pennsylvania in
Philadelphia. April 27, 2019.
Photo: Derek Rigby

some thoughts on inhospitality

DEBORAH ANZINGER, DANIELLE M. PURIFOY,
& DANIELLA ROSE KING
AN EDITED CONVERSATION
APRIL 27, 2019

To mark the opening of *Deborah Anzinger: An Unlikely Birth* I moderated a conversation between Anzinger and geographer and lawyer Danielle M. Purifoy. This marked a continuation of a collaboration between the three of us, who had been in conversation since 2018. Anzinger and I sought to engage Purifoy in a conversation around her experiences of environmental activism and reproductive justice; conversations that greatly impacted and inspired the exhibition and the discourse we developed around it. As well as contributing an essay to this catalog, Purifoy joined us on stage the day after Anzinger's exhibition opened. Titled "On Inhospitality," the event sought to explore notions and strategies of the *inhospitable*—a term borrowed from one of Anzinger's works in the exhibition. Below is an edited transcript of the discussion, that looked at historical struggles for emancipation, decolonization, and self-governance of the land and body throughout the black diaspora.

DANIELLA ROSE KING

DANIELLA ROSE KING

Today I'm hoping to discuss a number of issues inherent to the exhibition—including specific art works and their subject matter—as well as visual forms and vocabularies that Deborah has been developing throughout her practice. These include the use of certain materials and titles as potential apertures to speak about the urgencies of climate change, the Anthropocene, environmental racism, reproductive labor, and reproductive justice. I'm confident that *inhospitality* will provide a capacious lens through which a discussion can unfurl around place, space, the body, the land, the environment, history, and possible futures. *Inhospitable* is the title of a painting included in *An Unlikely Birth*, and has been a generative site of discussion for Deborah and I in the process of developing this exhibition. The term itself calls to attention relationships of subservience endemic to colonialism, plantation economies, and the economies that have developed in their wake, subverting the impulse/invective to welcome, accommodate, and defer to. I'm curious to hear from Danielle about how inhospitality resonates with your work as an environmental lawyer and geographer?

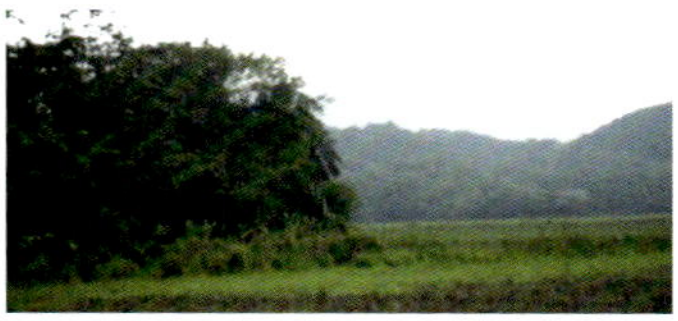

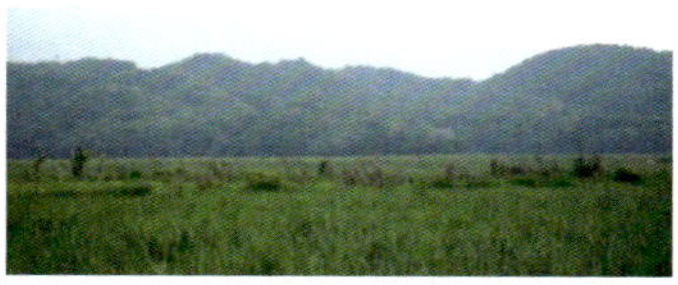

The Distraction of Symbolism, 2019. Video (still), color, sound, 7:00 minutes. Courtesy of the artist.

DANIELLE M. PURIFOY

I'm just really pleased and humbled to be here and thankful to my friends for showing up today. So, law and geography. I guess I should specify when I talk about geography because I think there is a sense of ... a very dominant sense of what geography is. Mapping, cartography, different landscapes. When I talk about geography I'm talking specifically about black geographies. So black spaces, intentional black spaces, like historic black towns and settlements in the United States, mostly in the south. And I'm also talking very much about local geographies. And a lot of these places have their origins, to sort of get at the theme of Deborah's work and of your curatorial work, on plantations. A lot of these black towns and settlements are actually at the site of former plantations that have been abandoned spaces or cast aside places where black folks have gathered and tried to create intentional, independent, political spaces for themselves. And in some cases tried to create their own kinds of economies. The way that the law intersects with these places is what I'm trying to think about. When people are trying to come together and to create a place, they want to use the tools of the law in order to protect that space, in order to set boundaries around that space, in order to set the rules of engagement in that space. My work argues that at least in the United States, the efforts of these black towns and settlements to utilize our dominant laws of our society

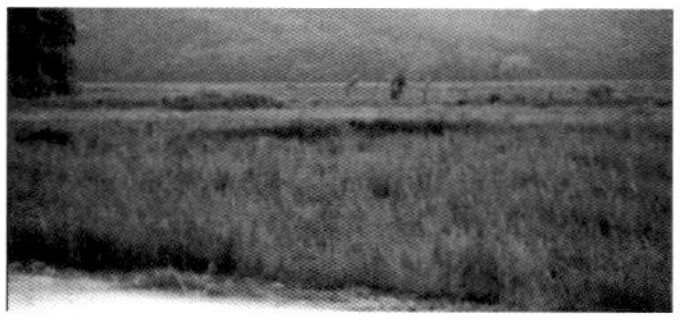

for regulating local space have been really fraught, and it's because of what we think of as structural racism, the laws and rules of our society that were set centuries ago, actually did not contemplate places like free black towns and settlements. So, the attempts of these communities to employ the laws to protect their spaces, in a lot of cases, from things like environmental dumping, importation of hazards, and total erasure has been really unsuccessful in a lot of ways. So, these communities have actually had to find not necessarily illegal but extra-legal ways of protecting themselves from ecological devastation. That's sort of the intersection.

DANIELLA ROSE KING

Could you talk about your understanding of environmental racism and some encounters with it in regards to the communities you've worked with?

DANIELLE M. PURIFOY

A lot of folks know about environmental racism from the 1980s, the sort of advent of what we know of as the United States Environmental Justice Movement, that actually started in my home state, North Carolina. And really, environmental racism has been defined historically as the systemic racial inequity in the distribution of environmental hazards, the disproportionate environmental burdens that black and brown and money-poor communities have had to bear as opposed to the kinds of environmental amenities enjoyed by mostly white folks and wealthy folks. The way that I think about environmental racism is really more in terms of the politics of development. So, if we think about how capitalism works and how places are developed, places are never developed in isolation. The kind of spaces that you think of as immaculate, well-appointed places are always built through a capitalist system on the backs of another place. So, there's some place that the waste from

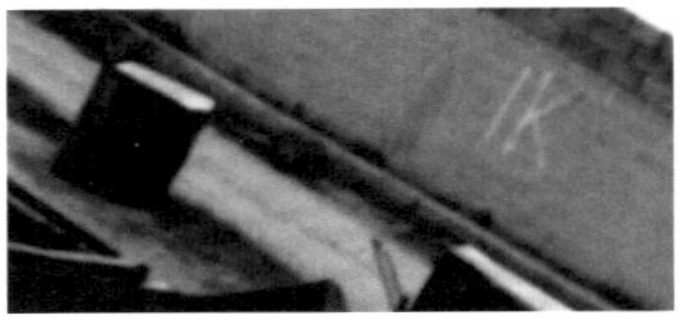

the construction has to go. There is some place that if there is water rights in contention, in order for this place to have all the water rights that it needs then that means that some other place has to lose it. And capitalism often works as a kind of zero sum game. And that has, as you can imagine, pretty devastating ecological impacts both locally and globally. For instance, most of the early environmental racism cases are around waste. Everything from municipal household waste to hazardous waste to nuclear waste. Who is bearing the brunt of the ecological and health impacts of that kind of waste? It goes far beyond that. It's about not only who is bearing the brunt of waste, and the hazards from coal fired power plants, from fracking, from oil and gas pipelines. We just had this huge, political movement at Standing Rock around the Dakota Access Pipeline. There's a similar battle that's happening in what we call North Carolina's Black Belt. It's the place in the state where plantation slavery was most heavily concentrated and has the highest concentration of black people in North Carolina. We have the Atlantic Coast Pipeline where there is a whole political battle about it being built right through those communities and the health impacts. So, those are some examples of the impacts. But that development is benefiting someone, it's benefiting a lot of these corporations, it's benefiting people in terms of the energy access but it's always at the expense of another community. So, I think about who is benefiting and who is being burdened by the way that we think about development and that's, I think, a really useful framework to think about in the moment where environmental justice and their movement around environmental racism starts. But really, these politics go way back, and they really go back to the plantation.

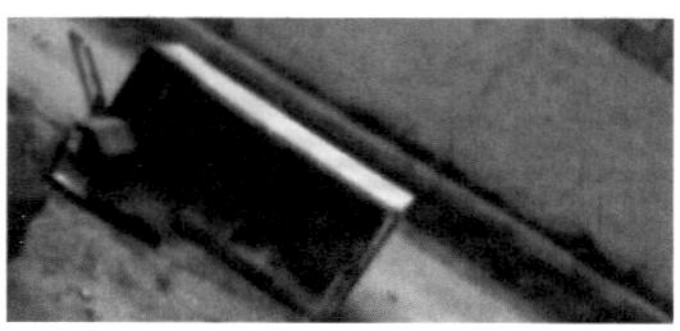

The Distraction of Symbolism, 2019. Video (still), color, sound, 7:00 minutes. Courtesy of the artist.

DANIELLA ROSE KING

It's a kind of terrible intersection of ... not necessarily an intersection but more a continuum of racial capitalism and plantation economies. The distribution of environmental and ecological hazards throughout the US is remarkably stark, it is akin to the deliberate and blunt process of redlining. Of course, this isn't limited to the US, as we see that generally in the "global south" including the Caribbean, these geographies are bearing the vast burden of environmental repercussions/consequences and catastrophes.

DEBORAH ANZINGER

I think about some of the points that Danielle is making regarding waste and how that actually intersects with the hospitality industry in Jamaica because when we lobby for cruise ships to dock (at Jamaica's ports) because we want the foreign currency from the cruise ships, at the same time where does the sewage get dumped from the cruise ships? That becomes part of the burden. To earn that foreign exchange, we take the sewage, which as you can imagine impacts the ecosystem, the coastal ecosystem and the coral reef ecosystem. So, I do think about that. Again, just to bring it back to inhospitality, and how hospitality becomes that burden.

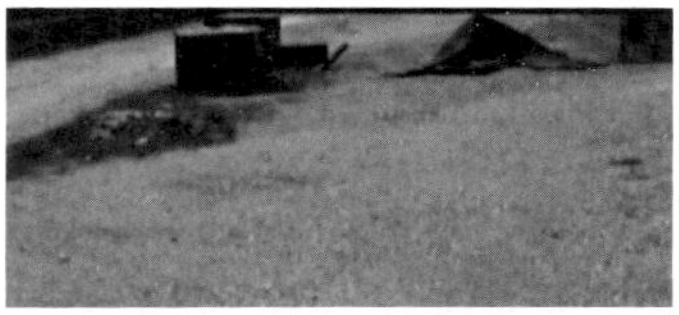

DANIELLA ROSE KING

Deborah, could you share a few words about the painting *Inhospitable*, that inspired this program? Its origins, meaning, and in relation to the conversation today?

DEBORAH ANZINGER

Well the work in terms of symbology etc., references the environment. I guess I think of inhospitality in this case as the quality of a space that is watching, observing, and has its own subjecthood. One of the other ways that inhospitality is addressed in the exhibition is through the installation *The Distraction of Symbolism* and the conversation that was recorded for the video. It's about how information about the environmental crisis we're dealing with is not accessible to the general public. I think spaces become more inhospitable with more access to that kind of information. I'm thinking about inhospitality as a means for survival, and as a means for thriving, and as a means for sustainability. And also thinking about hospitality—the legacy of hospitality—as the quality of space that is penetrated, mined from, or has to just bear the burden of whatever capitalistic developments are underway.

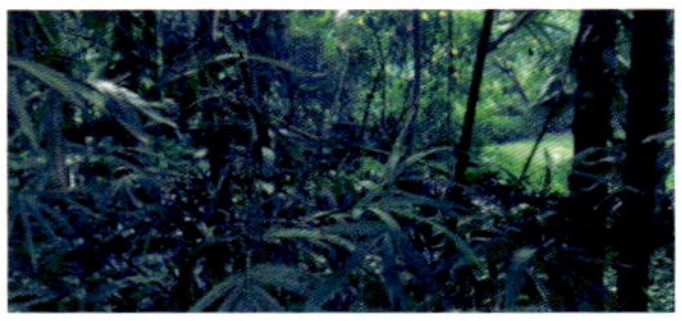

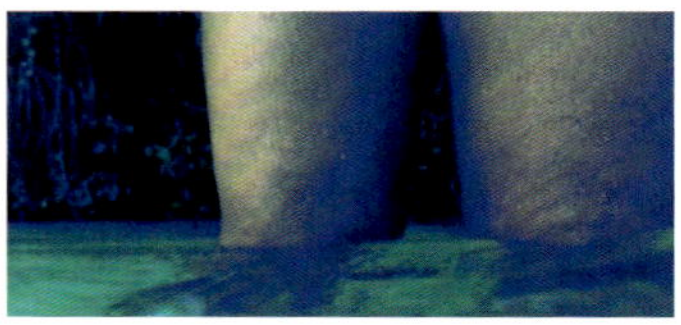

The Distraction of Symbolism, 2019. Video (still), color, sound, 7:00 minutes. Courtesy of the artist.

DANIELLE M. PURIFOY

Yeah. And I think that there's some work by folks to think of like the geographer—she's considered an honorary geographer—and black feminist scholar, Katherine McKittrick, about what it actually means, to dwell in those inhospitable spaces. How those places that we create narratives of deficit around actually have, by necessity, built the kind of tools and practices for bringing back their humanity, tools for liberation...These are things that we talk about a little bit abstractly in academia, and I think one way of making these more tangible is by looking at places that are in ecological crisis, places that have been the targets of hazardous burdens, places that are desperately impacted by climate change, and really observing what sort of practices are arising in those spaces. How do people survive in those spaces, how do people create communities in those spaces despite all of these things that are

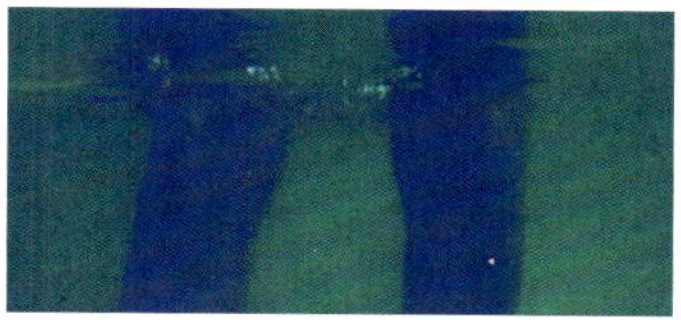

happening? I think this is how my work really connects not only to conceptualizations of the law, but to our relationship with the state, and to governance. These entities that we think of as trying to protect us are supposed to protect us in something that we try to call a democracy. Often in those particular spaces they're having to work completely outside of those structures. When they appeal to them through litigation, when they appeal to them through protest, when they appeal to them through voting administrations out and voting in new and extensively more progressive administrations—they are still saddled with the same kinds of burdens, no matter what the party. So, it's really important to think about those spaces as the most generative spaces for what the future actually has to look like. What is our future relationship to the government or the law or whatever if none of those tools are actually operating to protect or to save those particular spaces?

DANIELLA ROSE KING

Are there any specific examples that you could share with us about some of those approaches? Could we also think about some historical events, or communities that have been using inhospitality as a strategy for survival?

DANIELLE M. PURIFOY

Yeah. So one example—and I think these are examples we actually don't think of as examples of resistance against a state, or mechanisms of survival—is in a lot of the black towns and settlements that I've been to. A lot of them are what we call unincorporated spaces, so they don't have a separate municipal government. What ends up happening is in the absence of a kind of centralized government that is directly accountable to, or created by the state, these communities actually build their own kinds of political institutions. I think a lot about the church, for instance. You'll find in these places there's one thousand people with

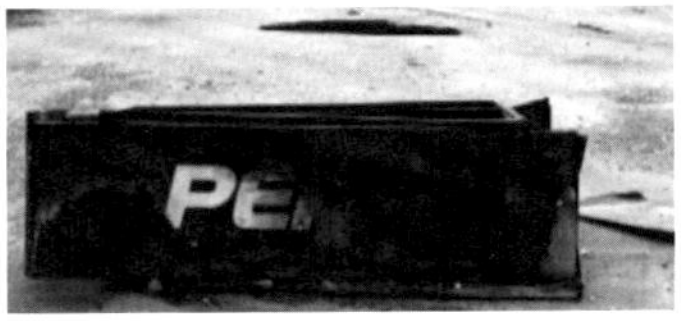

The Distraction of Symbolism, 2019. Video (still), color, sound, 7:00 minutes. Courtesy of the artist.

twenty churches, within a mile or two, and you're just like "wow, well people are just really religious or they must really be engaged or their churches must be really fractured." And it's typically not that. It's that the churches are actually serving different...providing different services for that community. There's a community that I always talk about that's in the center of North Carolina. It's outside of a historic white town. It used to be all the same plantation area, but this one part—they're actually several little communities—called West End (and it's an unincorporated black community) has been systematically denied access to wastewater sanitation infrastructure. They have a lot of challenges around raw sewage, a lot of challenges around illegal dumping in those spaces and extractive industry that is ringed around them. They have their churches operate as food pantries and schools. They've historically operated as recreation centers. They've operated—and really sort of created in the aggregate—the institutions that you think a small town might create. It's all private and you don't think of them as that, you think of these as civic organizations. But in the absence of a local government, this is what becomes the government. They often create something called community development corporations. You'll find them in a lot of places. These are a little bit more tied to government. They're non-profits that are supposed to be, were created for the express purpose, of trying to boost development in these perceived underdeveloped places, which are mostly black and brown places and indigenous places. Really what they end up functioning as is like micro governments in those spaces. There is a lot of discretion within those kinds of structures to really think about "what does it mean to build a local community that's accountable to each other, a secure community that has everything that it needs?" Even in the face of state repression and all sorts of other things, people have a real commitment to these places and to maintaining them in a particular way. It's remarkable to me because it really is happening. These are not places with police departments. These are not places with all of the regular infrastructure we see, but their relationships to one another are the things that are tying them together and continuing a community over, at this point, over one hundred and fifty years.

DEBORAH ANZINGER

Well the most clear or obvious example for me would be the Maroon Wars, the First and Second Maroon Wars that happened in the 1700s in Jamaica, which I think really set the tone for how the country has developed and to what degree capitalism has succeeded there. I mean you could say that part of the reason why Jamaica—as compared to somewhere like the Bahamas or Cayman Islands—doesn't have the same access to foreign exchange (which would mean that our dollar would be stronger) is really just a simple fact of the inhospitable nature of the country compared to our neighbors, to those specific neighbors. And a lot of that seems culturally tied to that history of the Maroon Rebellions and also the treaties that came out of the rebellions—which were a problem. The treaties were problematic. The treaties were won by the Maroons in the 1739 after about 11 years and after more British troops were poured or imported into the country to be able to penetrate the interior of the island. But the problem of the treaties was that after it was won, the negotiation that was made with the British was that in order to maintain that autonomy and to maintain the interior of the island as being separate from the constitution, that the Maroons would agree that any slaves that escaped from the plantations and made it up to the Cockpit Country would be returned by particular Maroon communities that were collaborating with the British. That said, it granted them autonomy and that space, the Cockpit Country, has remained a largely underdeveloped space. Importantly the space supplies most of the freshwater for the country, it's where a lot of important watersheds exist. To that degree, the country still remains what it's been historically called; which is the land of wood and water. A lot of us take for granted that freshwater is always accessible but there are quite a few Caribbean countries that don't even have rivers. Rivers are a precious commodity. I think about things like waste management and where exactly the waste goes. How many spaces are there that won't be contaminated by the waste of human settlement and agricultural livestock etc.? I think about how that maps on to the Cockpit Country, which is threatened right now but still largely provides most of the freshwater that we access.

DANIELLA ROSE KING

And it's amazing that inhospitality or the utilization of that by certain communities has had this political legacy as well as one of protecting the environment like you say, other Caribbean nations where the economy is completely dependent on tourism, it employs a third of the workforce and dictates the way the society is run as a result. This is combined with the privatization of land and resources and widespread ecological collapse. These realities call for drastically different conceptions of development. Deborah, could you say a few words about how your video installation *The Distraction of Symbolism*, 2019, attends to some of these issues?

DEBORAH ANZINGER

The installation consists of a dwelling referencing an architectural structure that you might call a shack. It's a structure that is not uncommon to find through rural or urban parts of Jamaica's parishes. I wanted to reference that particular structure because of the vernacular. It references a specific space, a specific geopolitical position that is a part of the everyday. Having visitors here able to access that space—which one can imagine as abroad, a foreign place where somebody else lives—I wanted it to be a space that, rather than hosting the curiosity or imagination of

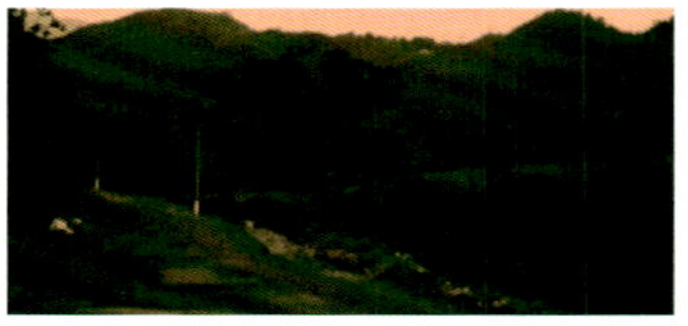

The Distraction of Symbolism, 2019. Video (still), color, sound, 7:00 minutes. Courtesy of the artist.

the visitor, it becomes a space of labor. With the presence of the plants, the trees provide this feeling of...a sanctuary. Though it's set up to resemble a sanctuary space, it doesn't function as a sanctuary space but rather as a space for the visitor to actually labor and listen. And that was a way of complicating the boundary between hospitality and inhospitality. Who is doing the labor and listening, and sort of overturning those dynamics? I wanted it to reference where it is right now, so we used native plants. And I also wanted it to be a space where you couldn't do anything to avoid being confronted by these specific accounts of the relationship between this current space and the space where I live or where that shack is referencing. So, while it is a space where you would visit, it's also a space for labor. I wanted that labor to come from the visitors whose curiosities were sort of being entertained.

DANIELLA ROSE KING

The video touches on some of the broader geopolitical specificities of waste, pesticides, and agriculture in Jamaica as well as the legacies of imperialism in terms of how lobbies function and the best interests of the country being put aside to the benefit of other geopolitical relationships. There's also mention of Marcus Garvey, black liberation movements and discussion of individual and communal responsibility in terms of climate change and the of use of pesticides, and the intertwinement of these issues. The radio show sampled in the work touches on a number of issues pertinent to other works in the exhibition and this conversation. Is there anything else from there you'd like to pull out for our discussion today?

DEBORAH ANZINGER

I'll briefly touch on a segment of the conversation. There are two sources of audio that are layered in the video. There is one source from interviews that I conducted with people who were inclined to answer questions I had in terms of their anxieties in their everyday lives about the environment and about their access to clean water and how aware they were of concepts of climate debt. That was layered on top of an Irie FM interview (on the program Africa Forum). I just happened to catch this segment where they were talking about Monsanto lobbying, and Bayer—Bayer and Monsanto are now owned by the same company, which of course is interesting because one is a pharmaceutical company and one is a company that's sort of poisoning the population. So, there's a nice cycle there. The host [Ka'bu Ma'at Kheru] was mentioning that for years she was on her program talking about the use of Monsanto's Roundup—which is now very well established as being toxic. Her father is a small farmer and she had no idea that while she was on this program talking about it that all of these farmers including her father were using this herbicide. So, the conversation then became about accessibility to information, and also how it is that small farmers and casual farmers are able to access this restricted chemical because Dr. Paul Ivey, who was her guest on the program says Roundup is listed under restricted chemicals and no one can access it without a license in particular industries. And the host is saying, "I've gone into the store and bought Roundup, I've done it." He's saying, "No, you can't." And she said, "I have." So, the argument goes on and finally he just has to say, "Okay, well there's probably a breakdown right there in the implementation." So, I really wanted to capture and use that particular part of the conversation because it demonstrates the lack of accessibility to information. And even if the information is accessible, who do you actually trust? Because if you can access this thing from the farm supply store, why would you think that it is something that's going to be killing you? So that's an example of what

The Distraction of Symbolism, 2019. Video (still), color, sound, 7:00 minutes. Courtesy of the artist.

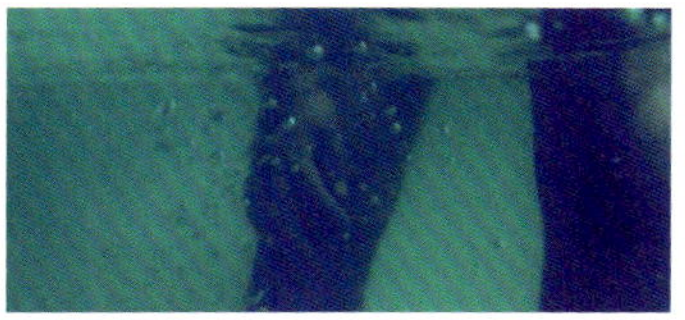

I would like to unpack from the audio. Two of the accounts reference this reliability and this sort of feeling of security that we have with freshwater in Jamaica, we assumed that it's going to be there because we're just so used to it. Then we had a drought, about three or four years ago, where it just wouldn't rain and we had never experienced that before. We had what was supposed to be hurricane season. Nothing happened during hurricane season. People associate hurricanes with disasters, of course, because we have these super hurricanes happening now after long periods of not having hurricanes. But hurricanes normally regenerate watersheds. So, when we've had what was supposed to be a hurricane season where nothing happens, as one of the people I interviewed said, "...people just had no water." People who had means, people from wealthier socioeconomic brackets, could go buy water and then everybody else, as she was saying, "I don't know what they were doing because they could not buy water." I use that particular part because in some ways it foretells what could happen in the geopolitical north where it's always assumed there is enough land and resources. The first places that are feeling that fallout from these climate changes are spaces like Jamaica, spaces like the Caribbean, Africa, etc., places that have been historically mined for the colonial project or the capitalism project. The video also illustrates how imperialism continues even though we have this sort of symbolic national independence. All of these countries and nations had this symbolic independence in the 1960s that sort of swept across the globe. But imperialism continues. One of the things the host was saying was that Jamaica, in theory, has a vote at the table with what she referred to as the "one world food order." But Jamaica essentially has to ... Jamaica's hand is forced to vote along with the United States because of ... dependence on the United States for energy...fossil fuel, etc.

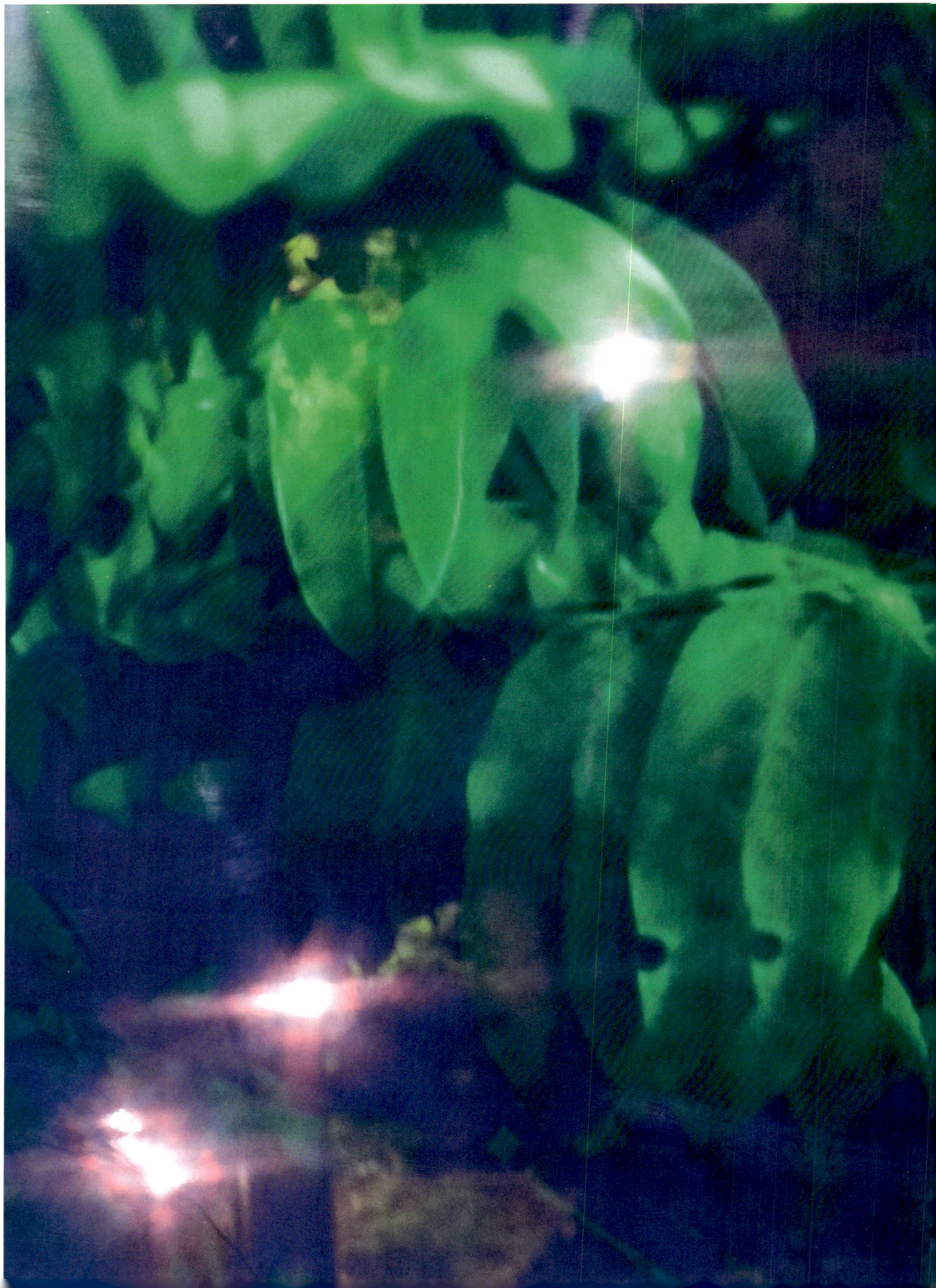

The Distraction of Symbolism, 2019. Video (still), color, sound, 7:00 minutes. Courtesy of the artist.

DANIELLA ROSE KING

There was a text that really drew Deborah and I both to your work, Danielle: "On the Stubborn Whiteness of Environmentalism." In it you talk about how communities throughout the black diaspora and the "global south" are those that are most readily dealing with the effects of climate change, waste, and pollution, yet the narrative around climate change is being driven from the geopolitical control centers of the Northern hemisphere. It's a really important text, so thank you for it!

It is my sincere hope that my curatorial practice accommodates and highlights black feminist approaches and critiques and testimony that feeds into that discussion. But as bleak as the reality seems to be, about environmental degradation, and its origins in the slave trade and the stubborn resilience of oppression, I don't want to be completely hopeless. So I wonder what are some of the narratives or stories or examples that give you hope and that ... you're trying to highlight and amplify through your own work?

DANIELLE M. PURIFOY

It's really hard to—I will say, I am hopeful. I came up in a School of Environment, that's what I have my Ph.D. in and I've only been out a year, not even a year. One of the things, even as I was going through that program, that I realized is that environmentalism will not save us. That was part of the impetus for writing that piece. And because one of the struggles that I had, while I was going through this program, was why are we never actually talking about the themes which are the reason I came to this program? I thought that this was the place where you went to actually learn what can we do within these communities. What tools do we have to actually meaningfully protect these communities? I went to law school before that thinking "Hey maybe the law, maybe environmental law will get us there?" I think my hope is kind of rooted in a final letting go

The Distraction of Symbolism, 2019. Video (still), color, sound, 7:00 minutes. Courtesy of the artist.

we talk about the devastation of climate change, people are forced to migrate, internally within the United States you see that happening, in a lot of these historic black communities. When a lot of these places came off (and this is historical), when a lot of these places that came off of the plantation were established, they were given the low-lying land; these are the areas that flood. These are areas that are the most prone to ecological devastation just by virtue of their topography. So, that's without mining; that's without dumping; that's without any of the other ecological devastation that's accrued to those spaces over the last one hundred and fifty years. And we're seeing ... So, I got ... For instance, I got my start in this work after Hurricane Katrina. I was working in Louisiana for about three years on the recovery and really started to notice, who was able to come back, structurally: who was able to access the resources, even if they had insurance, to actually come back to that city? I was talking with black folks who were displaced. Their entire family, generations of their family lived in New Orleans. They don't have any family outside of Louisiana. So now they're stranded in a place that might as well be a different country. "I'm in Las Vegas stranded in a community that I don't know and I actually can't find a way to give back because I don't have enough money and I had insurance but they want me to match, they want me to provide a match for the insurance payout in order to actually access the money that I would need to rebuild, which is not even enough to begin with." So, yeah, a lot of those stories over and over and over again resonating within the United States and I think one of the fantastic things about being in conversation today is the connectivities are just so direct. What's happening in Jamaica in terms of food and agriculture is part of what's happening in black agricultural spaces in the Southern United States that have been totally wiped out with land loss in the advent of these big Ag[riculture], like thirty, forty years ago. So, we can see very clearly the connectivities and then how they lead to these ecological devastations that are contributing to these climate impacts that we have both embedded within and outside of the country.

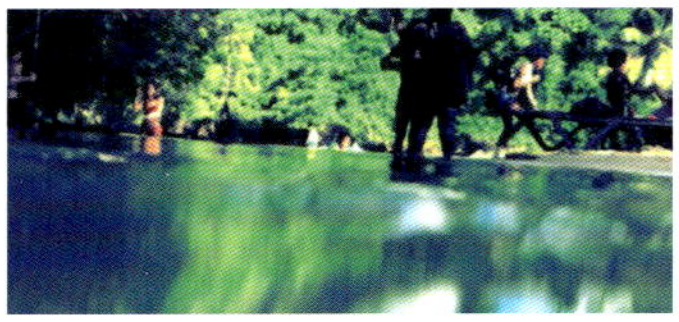

The Distraction of Symbolism, 2019. Video (still), color, sound, 7:00 minutes. Courtesy of the artist.

DANIELLE M. PURIFOY

I think one of the things that's really striking is how these happenings, like in Jamaica, and these conversations is how they are really resonant with a lot of the conversations I'm having with folks in these [black American] communities. And even though we are definitely within the United States, these are spaces that benefit—and all of us who are here benefit from the United States as an imperial project, there's no question about it—and simultaneously everyone is not benefiting in the same way, and the internal dynamics of this country mean that there are colonies within this country. We've talked about them, most notably indigenous nations, but the positionality of black folks in this country, can also manifest in those same particular ways. One of the ways is when black communities (like these communities that I'm working with) actually try to assert some form of even local political independence, you can see very clearly that the entitlements, the political and legal entitlements that you might expect as a so-called "United States citizen" just do not accrue in the same kinds of ways. What that means, geographically, what it means in terms of climate change, or water access, is a lot of these communities don't drink their water. Some because they actually don't have water flowing through their pipes—their wells have gone dry because they've been sucked up by the local landfill that is using the water to control the mounting waste. We've had several cases like that where people who had water all of a sudden just don't. But the folks in a lot of the communities that I work with the most they don't drink their water because of the contamination. This is something that the community knows and so they're doing what I imagine folks of means did in Jamaica during the drought: they're finding bottled water, they're paying tons and tons of money for bottled water. They take the risk of bathing, and showering and stuff like that, with the water that's there but they're like "it's weird, I'm bathing in it but I won't ingest it but I am ingesting it because it's going in my skin." There's just all of these negotiations. Then also when

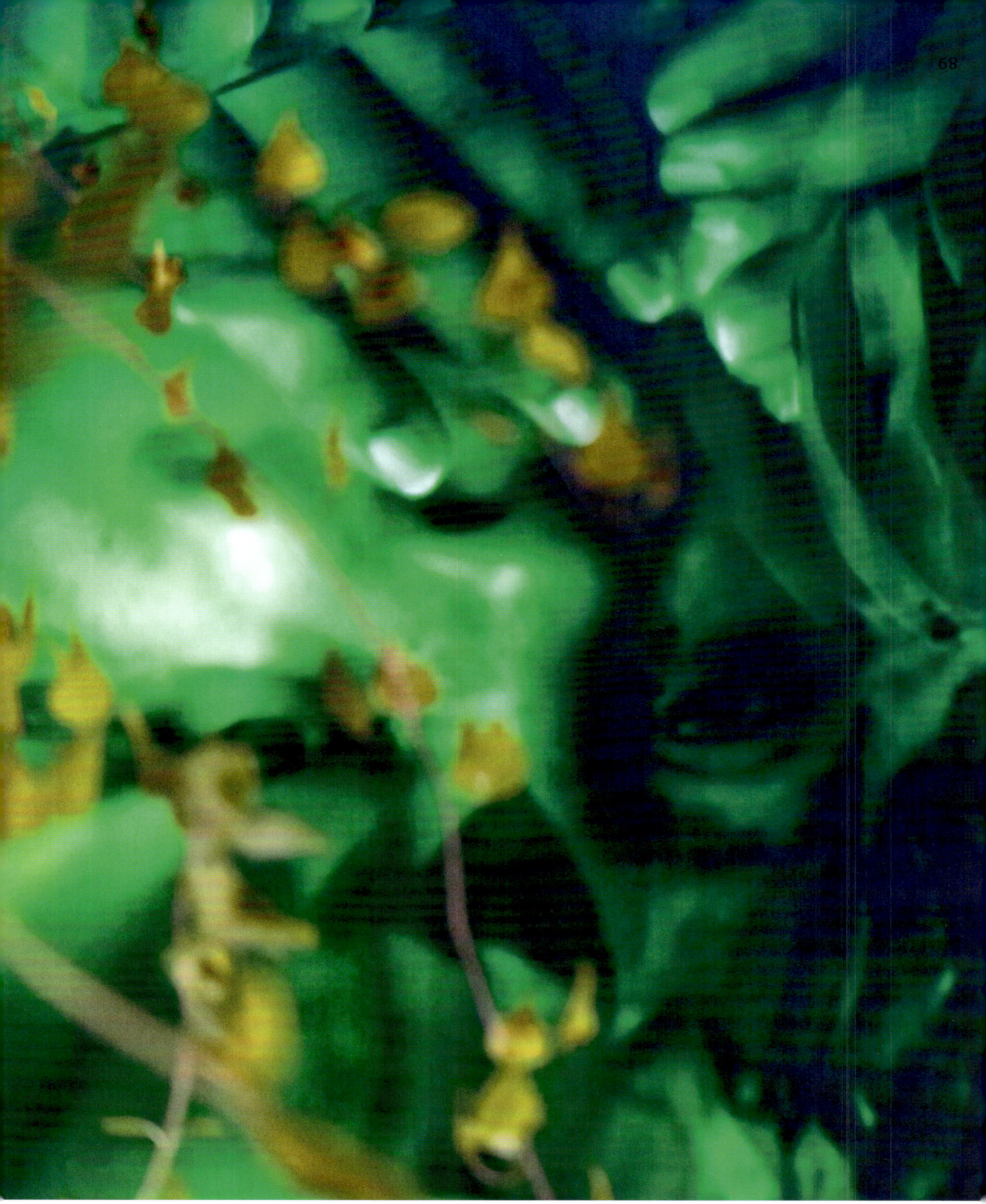

that those are the things that will help. So, what it means—and I think this is rooted in a black feminist tradition—is that we can come up with and think for ourselves about what actually works. What is it that we actually need? And we don't have to be rooted in these sort of conceptualizations or these practices that have been imposed on us because we actually know that for a lot of reasons that I won't go into (unless you have questions about it), that the ways that we have put forward to protect the environment have only functionally really protected white communities (and not even all white communities). So, it's really been important to set that aside and say, "what are the traditions within which black and brown and indigenous folks have always been able to protect themselves and sustain themselves?", and that really means in a lot of ways going back to very, very, very old traditions. That means actually really questioning capitalist development ideologies, this sense of a linear progress narrative that with every technology that we're building that we're only getting better, and that we're only elongating our lives, and we're only protecting ourselves more. I think that we can start to undermine those narratives and really start to think about: well what has kept us safe? What has kept us healthy? What practices do we want for ourselves? And I think really what it does is removes us from— thinking about the example of the conversation in your video Deborah—the sense that a technological fix will come along and somebody will invent something to get rid of this problem that we now have because of some other technological innovation. No, it's on us building relationships with each other. It's on us *actually* conceptualizing the kind of society we want to live in that will *actually* get us closer to what will *actually* protect us. And that is deeply within a black feminist tradition, by necessity, because black women, hierarchically in this society, and globally, have always been at the bottom of the barrel and those people who are at the bottom, those people who are in the spaces that are inhospitable, have to be, by necessity—they're the least served by the existing system so they are the ones that are tasked with coming up with "what we do to survive, and what we do to get ourselves

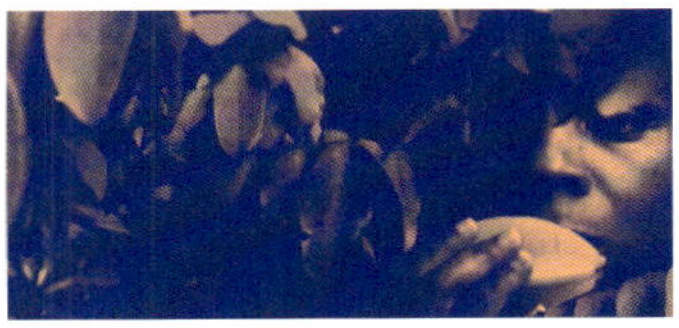

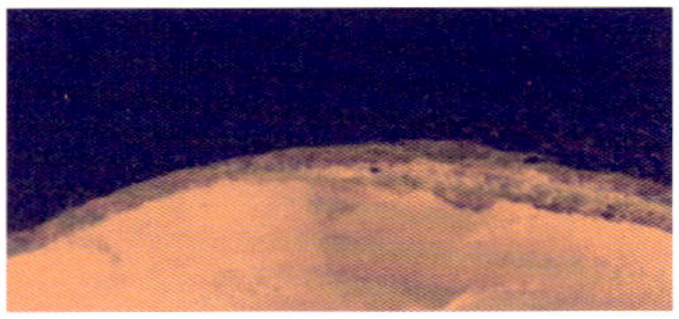

The Distraction of Symbolism, 2019. Video (still), color, sound, 7:00 minutes. Courtesy of the artist.

to a place where we can actually thrive?" That's the sort of thing that gives me hope. Not only that , but also that a lot of other people are actually starting to come to terms with that. It's not just me, isolated in the corner—there is a whole bunch of people who are like, "Yeah man, we can't do this anymore. We can't do this like this anymore, and actually we're going to have to talk to each other, and we're going to have to actually think about what we can do to take care of each other and be accountable to each other and to our communities in a particular way that means that I can no longer just be over here thinking I'm in this silo developing this thing, and not think about everything else that's happening." Yeah, so that's kind of what gives me hope. There's hope in the hopelessness of what we have right now.

DEBORAH ANZINGER

I get ... No, I one hundred percent agree with everything Danielle said. I guess I'll just add one small thing: redefining what it means to thrive, and what we think of as sustainable, because a lot of what we determine or define as thriving is actually rooted in these definitions that were created through capitalism.

DANIELLA ROSE KING

Absolutely. I'm going to ask one more question then I'd love to open it out to the audience, which was to think about ... I know that you're doing some research towards this Danielle. But looking at the intersection of the environment and reproductive justice, I couldn't help but think ... Of course, I'm thinking about this for lots of reasons. But within the exhibition and just when you were thinking about ... when you were describing scientific approaches and our perceptions of progress and of yeah, what it means to try and reproduce our present in perpetuity. If there's some way that reproductive justice kind of fits in there.

DANIELLE M. PURIFOY

Yeah. So, I think of reproductive justice as a movement (and I'm most familiar with the black feminist's approaches to it) to think about what it means to actually have a future in which black people are not dying in the ways that they are dying right now. How do you actually produce a black future that we want to really be in? I think that's a really important question not only for people who are having families, not only for people who can bear children, or want to bear children but also just for our society at large. So, I see reproductive justice as really deeply embedded in the politics of what we think of now as environmental racism and in terms of capitalism—I mentioned the term racial capitalism—these things are very deeply intertwined. Our development politics are deeply racialized, that is what produces what we call environmental racism. What that means is that in order to get to the black future—that black feminist reproductive justice organizers are thinking about—we cannot continue in this current system. Then there are also very, very practical things about the ways in which what happened to our environments, what we are exposed to, impacts our ability to reproduce. That's a starting point for thinking about this, that your actual ability to reproduce is (like all of ours, but disproportionately, black and indigenous women's ability to reproduce) is very much tethered to what is happening in their immediate environments. And it's not just about ecologically what's happening, or in terms of hazards and all of those sorts of things, it's also about the stresses of racism. It's about all sorts of other things that feel more intangible but that actually have tangible burdens on our bodies. So yeah, I really do think about these things and I'm doing research about all the ways in which folks are trying to get more in touch, folks who are working in this realm of reproductive justice are getting a lot more in touch with this.... I find a lot of those folks are becoming doulas. People are really thinking about how do we disengage from this hospital-driven, pharmaceutical-driven approach to reproduction? Part of that has to do

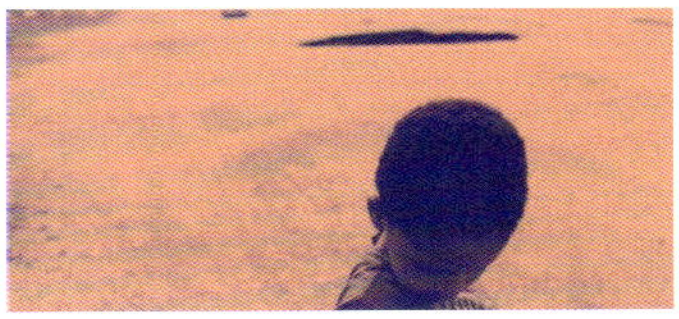

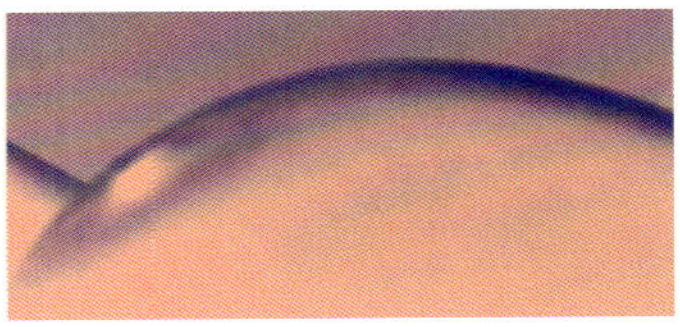

with—maybe you all remember what happened to Serena Williams when she was having her child—people's fear that "I've had a healthy pregnancy and now I'm entering into this space, and I'm endangered, I'm not getting the actual care that I need. What can I do?" This is, again, re-conceptualizations that go back to old practices. How do we reproduce in a way, and have babies in a way that we know that we're taken care of—that we know we're being taken care of by people who understand the risks that we may be under and then also care enough about us in this process? So, I think there's dual things that are happening, there's the kind of ideological "Okay, well for us to get here, some of our practices have to change. What about this old practice? What about this practice of midwifery or whatever? Let's see what that does. Let's actually think about, again, things that require more tangible, non-instrumental relationships to one another." So that's how I think about those two things together. I'm in the very early stages of the research for this but I'm excited to write and talk more about it.

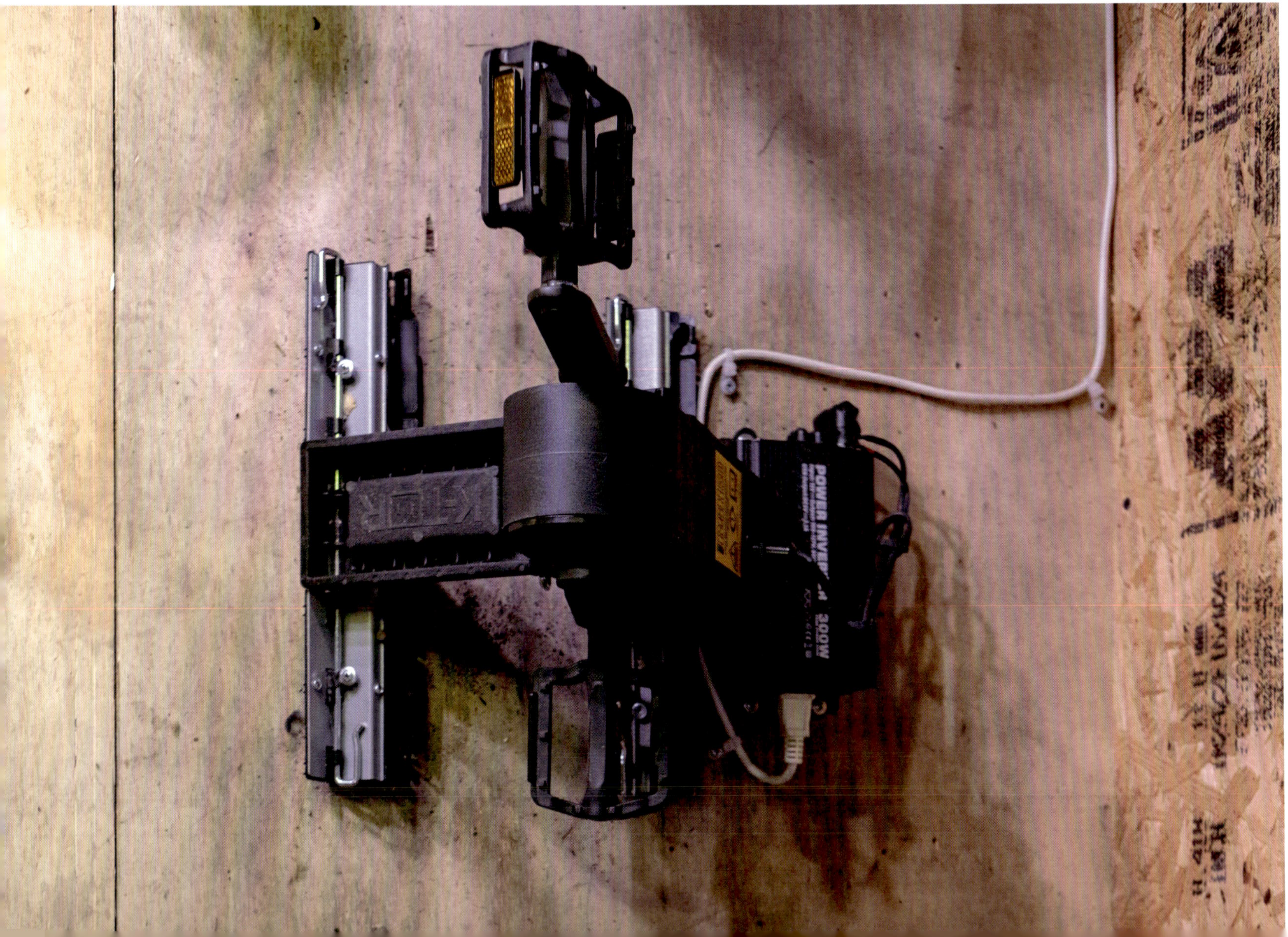

The Distraction of Symbolism (detail), 2019. Courtesy of the artist.

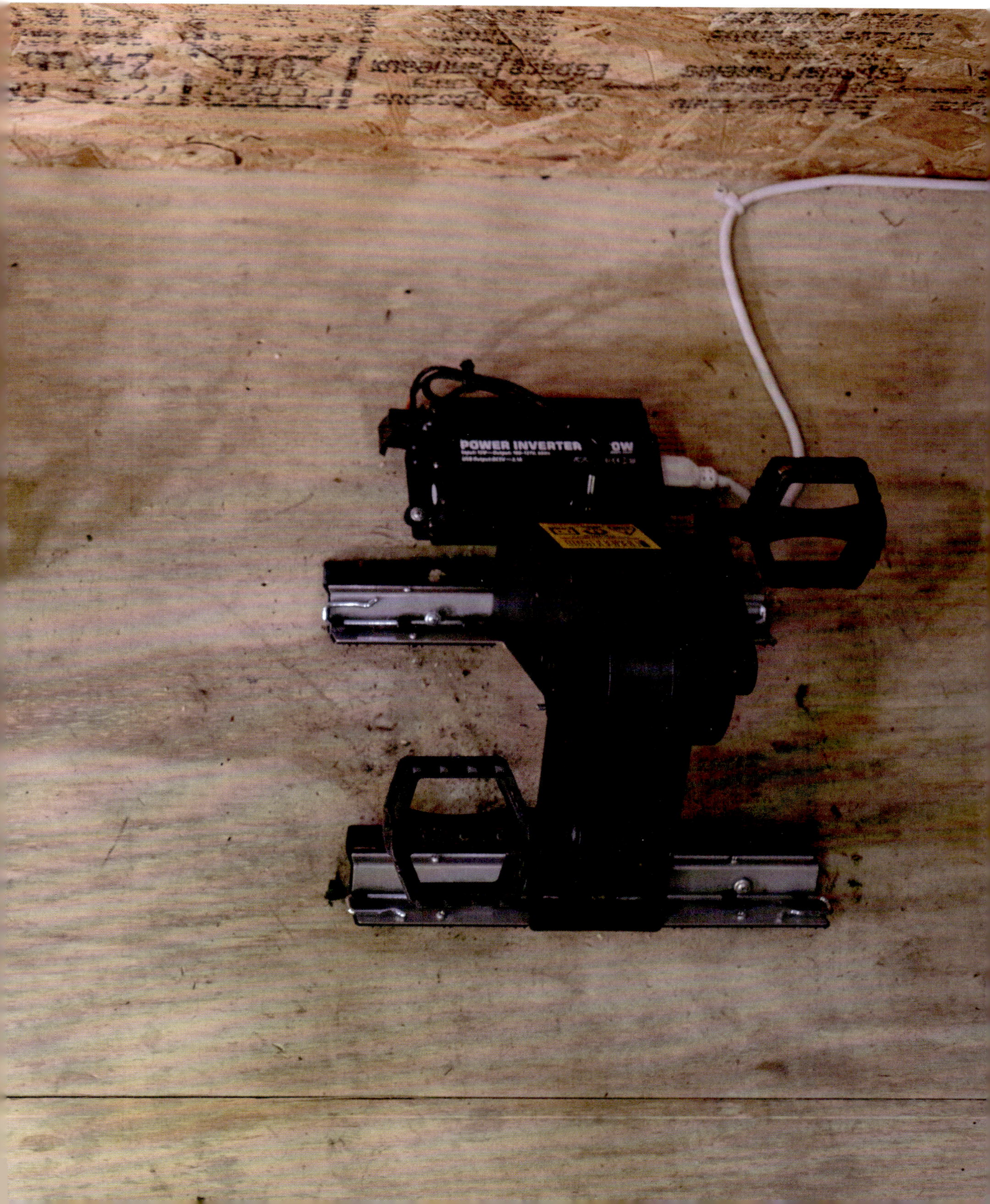
POWER INVERTER

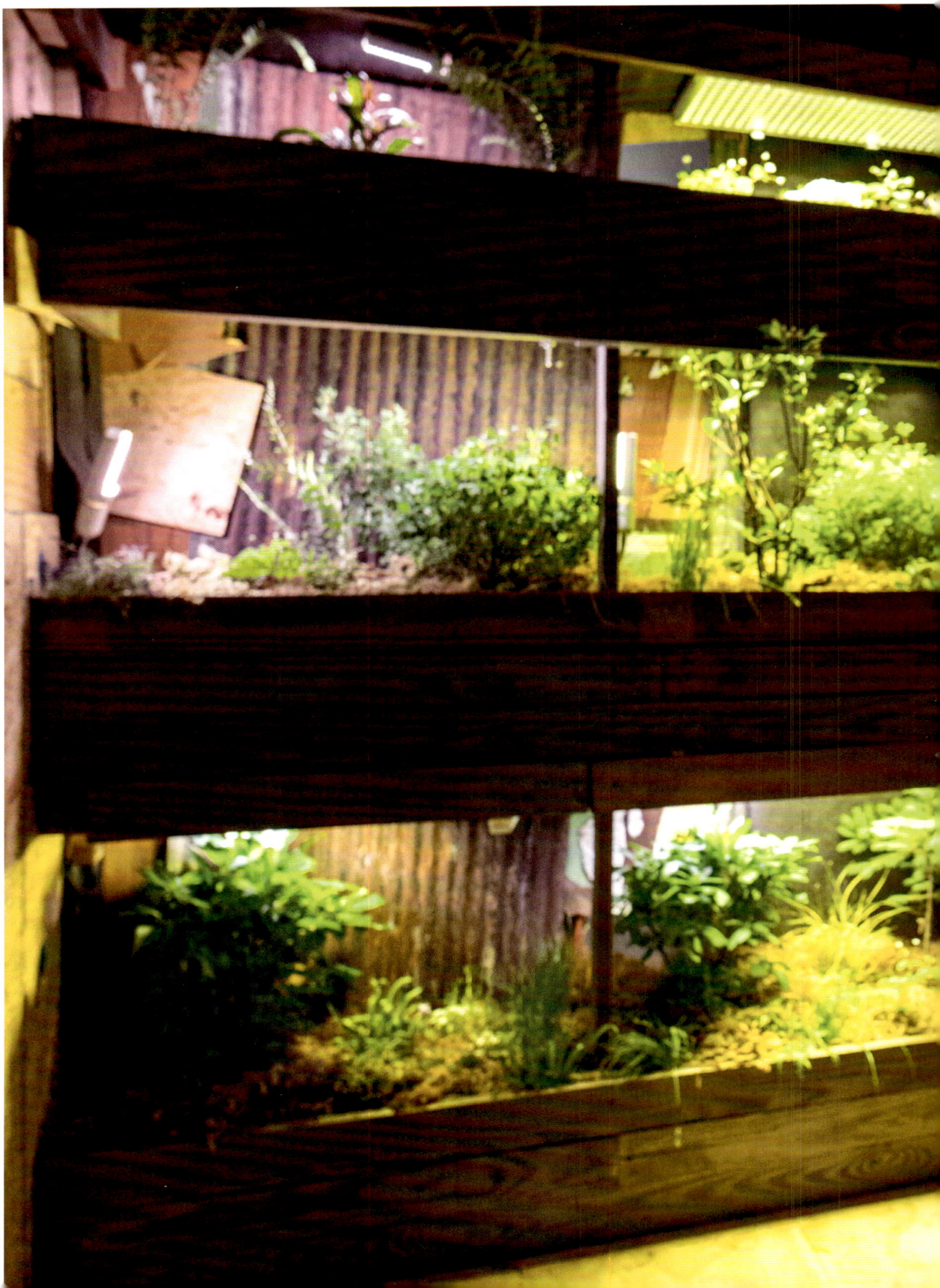

The Distraction of Symbolism (detail), 2019. Courtesy of the artist.

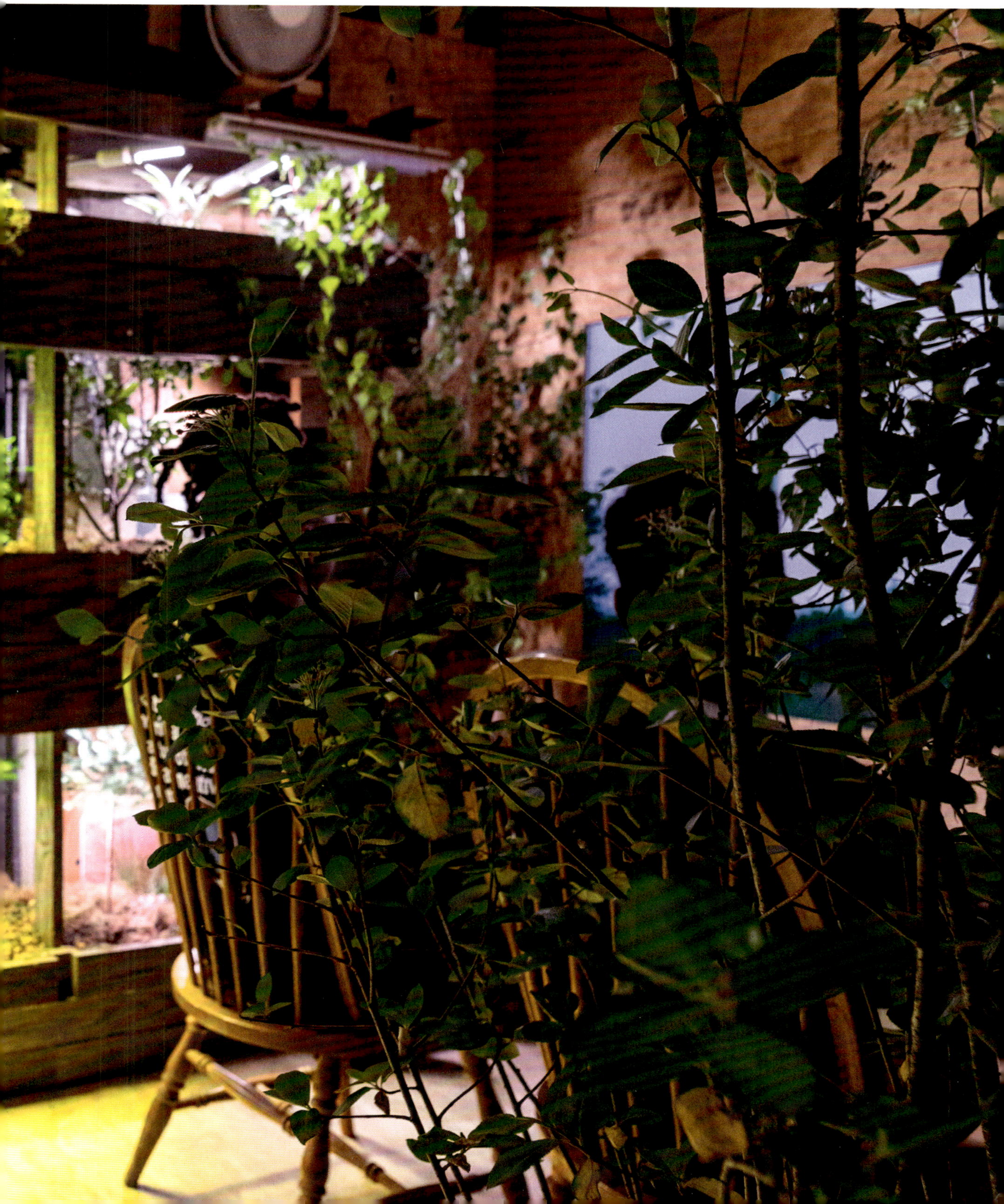

The Distraction of Symbolism (detail), 2019. Courtesy of the artist.

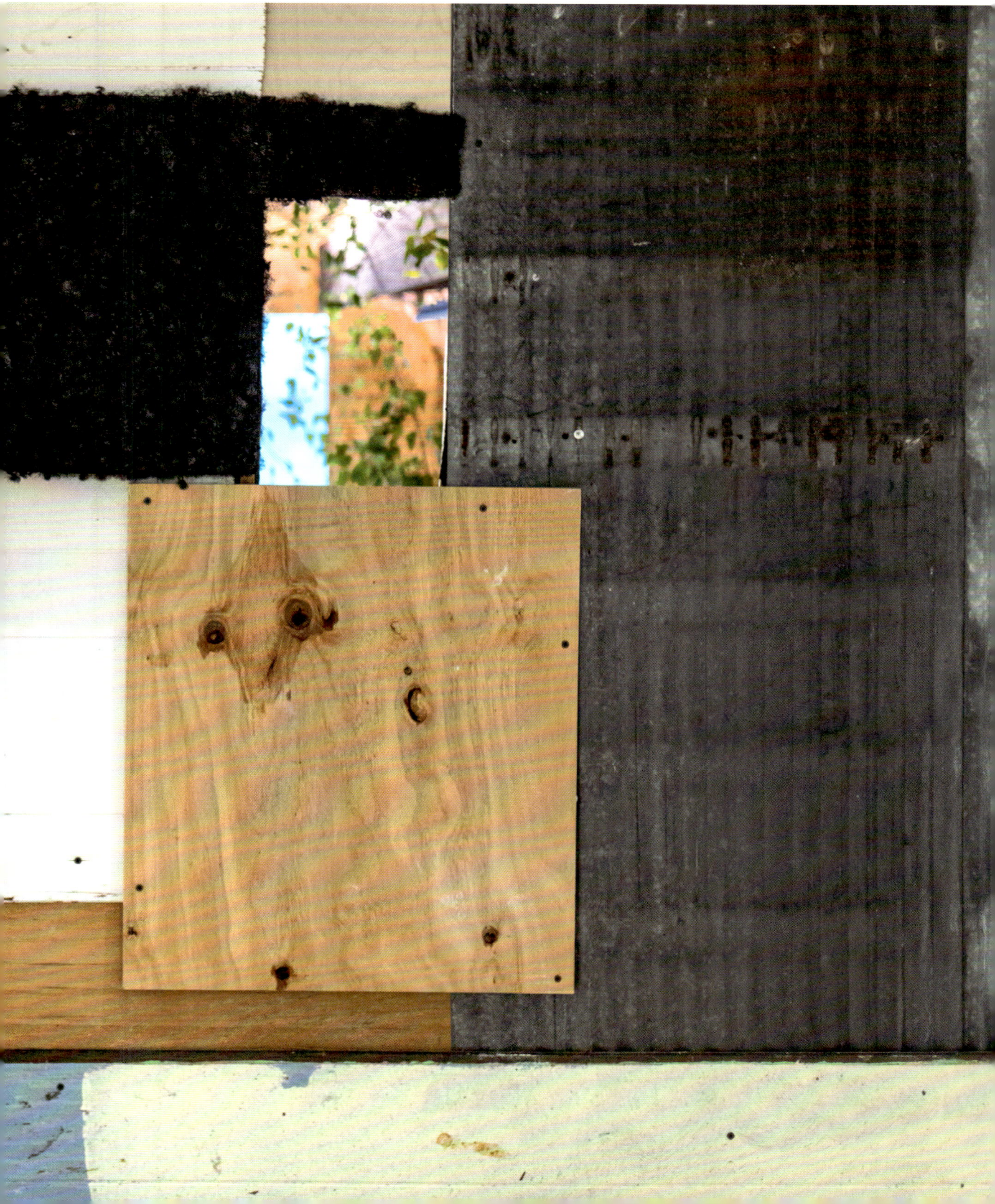

works on paper

Growth Index #1, 2019. Courtesy of the artist.

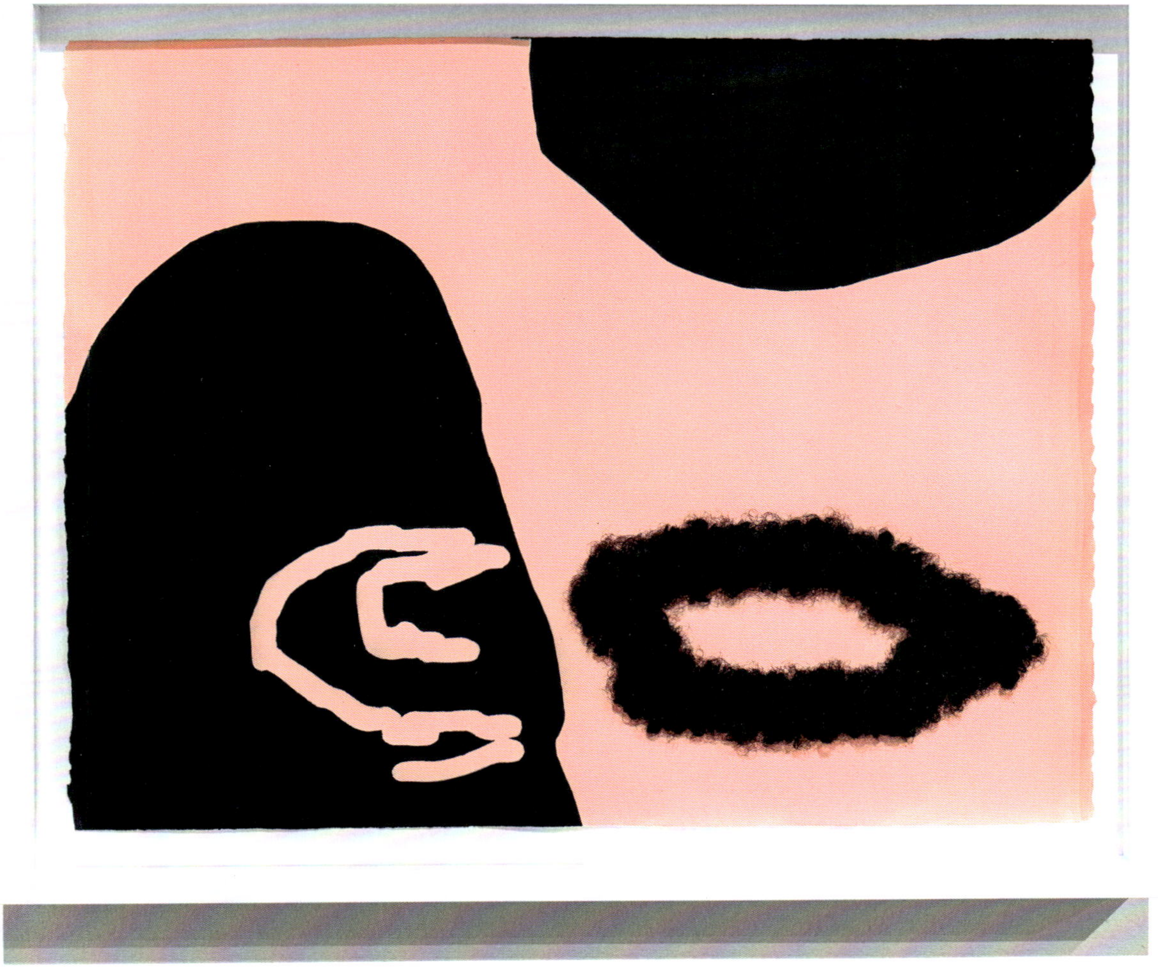

Growth Index #2, 2019. Courtesy of the artist.

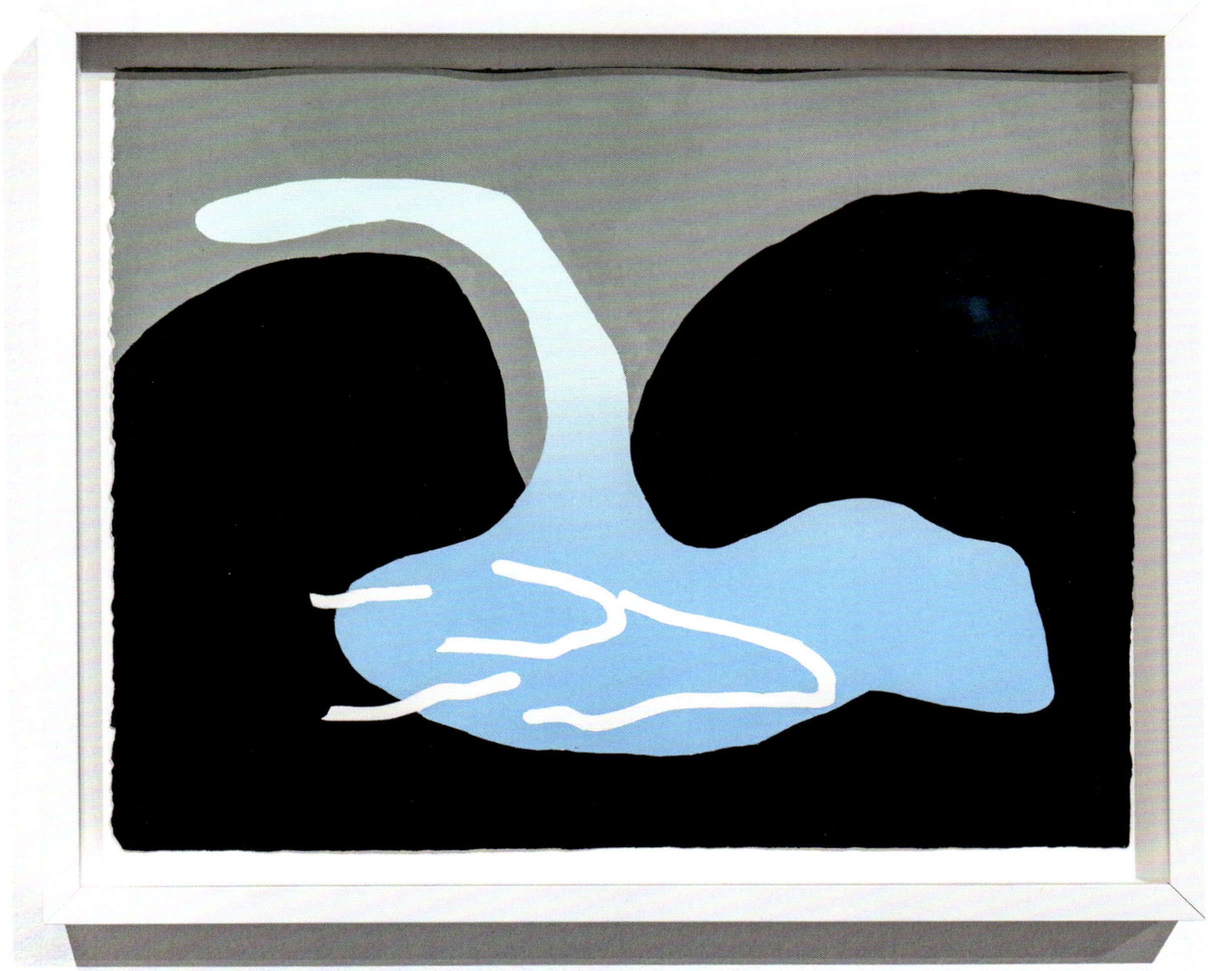

Growth Index #3, 2019. Courtesy of the artist.

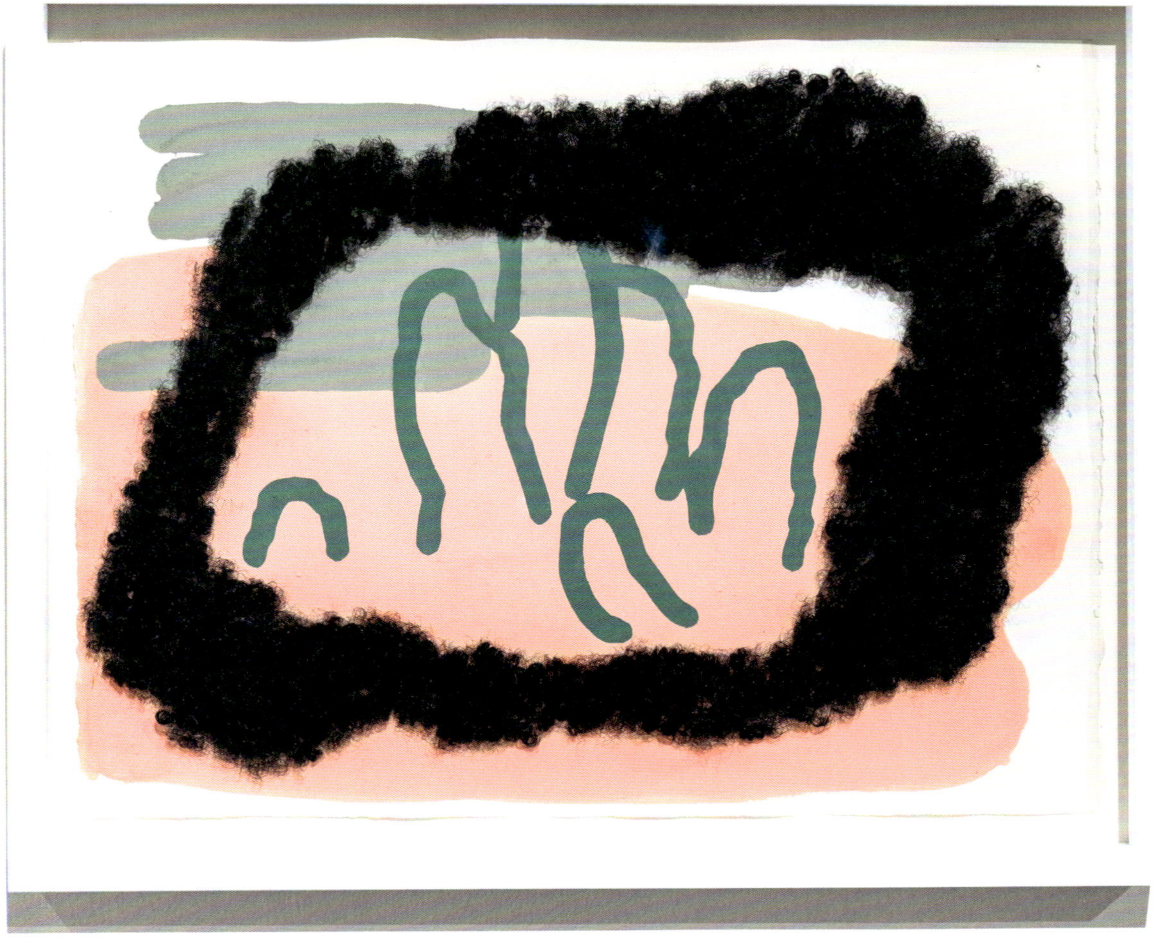

Growth Index #4, 2019. Courtesy of the artist.

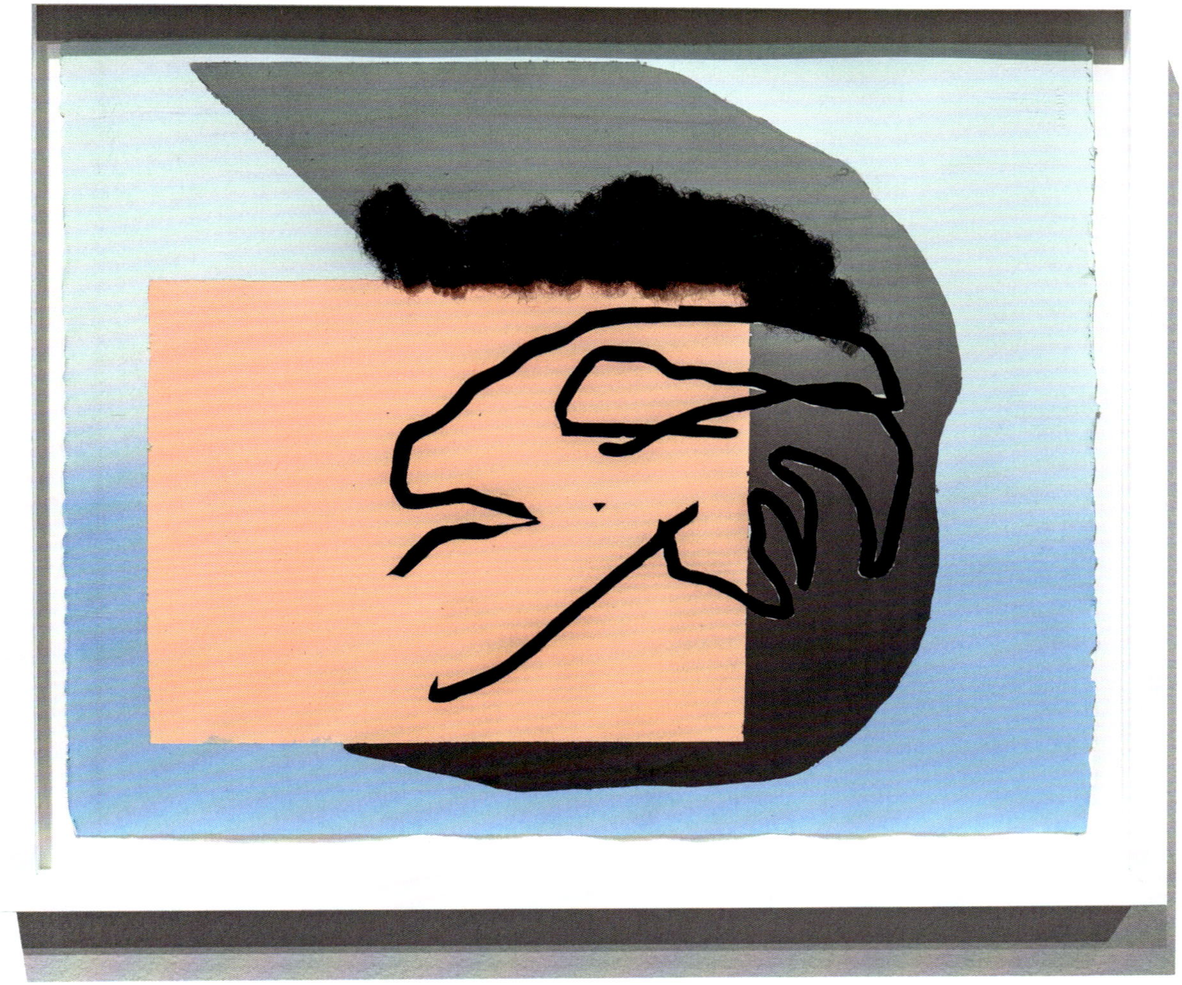

Growth Index #5, 2019. Courtesy of the artist.

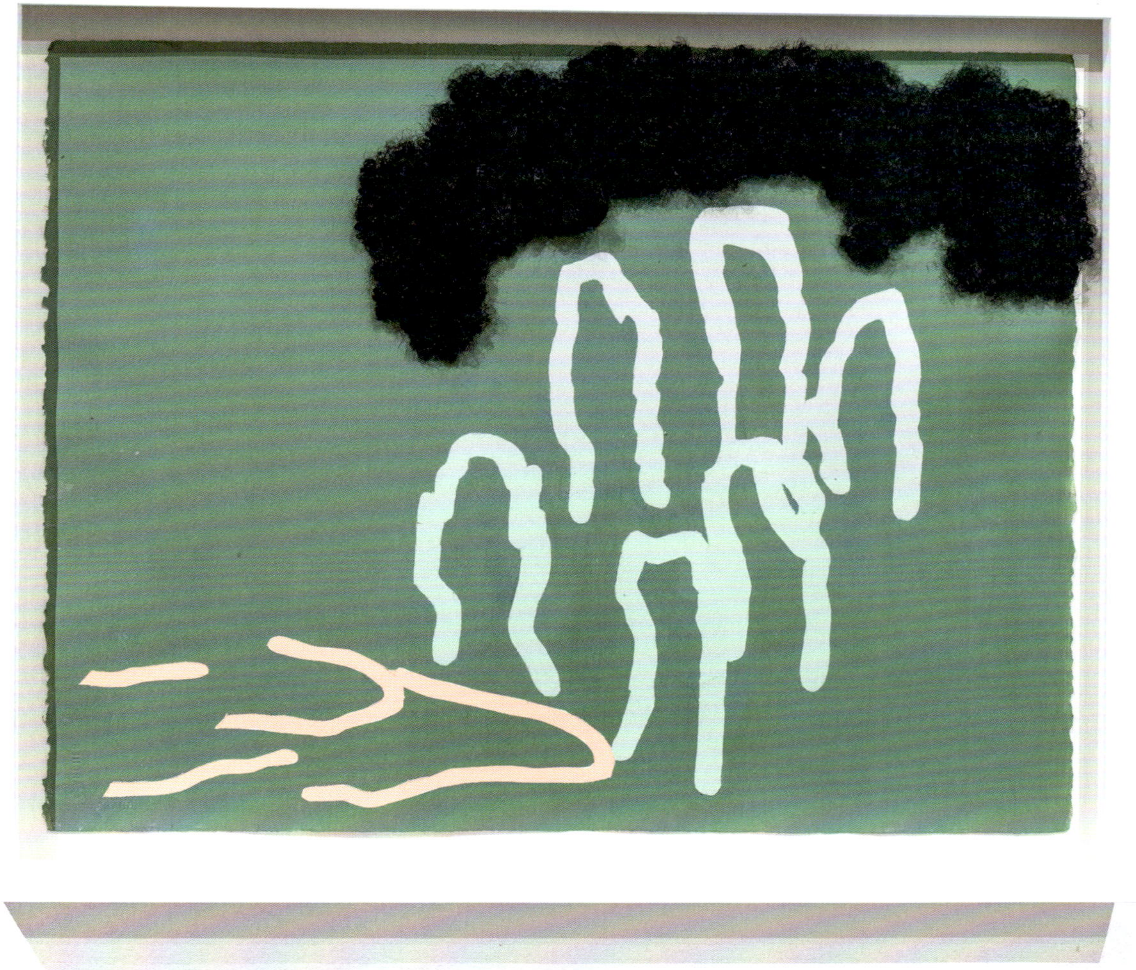

Growth Index #6, 2019. Courtesy of the artist.

CHECKLIST

An Unlikely Birth, 2018
Acrylic, mirror, Aloe barbadesis, and synthetic hair on canvas and Styrofoam
80 × 131 inches
Courtesy of the artist
pg 44–49

Garden, 2018
Acrylic and synthetic hair on canvas
81 × 59 inches
Courtesy of private collection
pg 51

Inhospitable, 2018
Acrylic, mirror, and synthetic hair on canvas
68 × 54 inches
Courtesy of the artist
pg 53–55; 124–125

Soaked In Shade, 2018
Mirror and acrylic on ceramic
48 × 12 inches
Courtesy of the artist
pg 57

Sprout, 2019
Acrylic on ceramic
Four pieces: approximately 5 × 10 inches
Courtesy of the artist
pg 59

Resonant, 2017
Acrylic on ceramic
20 × 14 × 3 inches
Courtesy of the artist
pg 60–61

Fiction As A Vessel For Reality, 2016
Aloe barbadensis and acrylic on ceramic
12 × 12 × 4 inches
Courtesy of the artist
pg 62

Eye #2, 2019
Acrylic on ceramic
Three pieces: approximately 4 × 10 inches each
Courtesy of the artist
pg 63

I Told You, 2016
Acrylic and mirror on canvas
72 x 54 inches
Courtesy of the artist
pg 65

Before you realized you could be seen, I watched you soaked in the shade while I was conceiving, 2018
Acrylic, mirror, and synthetic hair on canvas
72 × 54 inches
Courtesy of the artist
pg 67

Unfeed, 2019
Acrylic on ceramic
28 × 17 × 3 inches
Courtesy of the artist
pg 68

The Distraction of Symbolism, 2019
Installation: mixed materials, plants, lights, K-TOR® power units, video, color, sound, 7:00 minutes
Courtesy of the artist
pg 30–34; 72–103

Growth Index #1, 2019
Acrylic and synthetic hair on paper
16 × 20 inches
Courtesy of the artist
pg 107

Growth Index #2, 2019
Acrylic and synthetic hair on paper
16 × 20 inches
Courtesy of the artist
pg 109

Growth Index #3, 2019
Acrylic and synthetic hair on paper
16 × 20 inches
Courtesy of the artist
pg 111

Growth Index #4, 2019
Acrylic and synthetic hair on paper
16 × 20 inches
Courtesy of the artist
pg 113

Growth Index #5, 2019
Acrylic and synthetic hair on paper
16 × 20 inches
Courtesy of the artist
pg 115

Growth Index #6, 2019
Acrylic and synthetic hair on paper
16 × 20 inches
Courtesy of the artist
pg 117

CONTRIBUTOR BIOGRAPHIES

DEBORAH ANZINGER

(born Kingston, Jamaica; lives Kingston) works in painting, sculpture, and video at the intersection of black feminist, environmental, and geopolitical interrogation. She employs nontraditional materials such as living plants, afro-kinky hair, and mirrors as openings to intimate and alternative aesthetics of being in the world. Anzinger's work has been exhibited at the National Gallery of Jamaica, Kingston; the Museum of Contemporary African Diasporan Art, Brooklyn; the Royal West of England Academy, Bristol; the National Art Gallery of the Bahamas, Nassau City; and Sargent's Daughters, Nicelle Beauchene Gallery, and 47 Canal, all in New York. *Deborah Anzinger: An Unlikely Birth* is her first US museum solo exhibition. A 2018 recipient of the Pollock-Krasner Grant, Anzinger founded New Local Space, a contemporary visual art initiative in Kingston that provides a place for artists to experiment with new ideas, collaborate with each other, and engage with the public.

DANIELLA ROSE KING

is a London-born and Philadelphia-based writer, curator, and producer and the Whitney-Lauder Curatorial fellow at the Institute of Contemporary Art, a position she has held since 2017. Her last exhibition at ICA, *The Last Place They Thought Of*, was a group exhibition of four women artists that investigated how geographical, ideological, and spatial paradigms determine and reproduce uneven social relations.

As an independent curator she curated *On Visibility and Camouflage: Black Women Artists for BLM* at We Buy Gold in Bedford-Stuyvesant, Brooklyn in 2017; *On Limits: Estrangement in the Everyday* at The Kitchen, NY in 2016. King was the 2015–2016 Whitney Independent Study Program Helena Rubinstein Curatorial Fellow. King has held institutional positions as Assistant Curator at Nottingham Contemporary; Program Curator at MASS Alexandria, Egypt; Exhibitions and Events Manager at Iniva, London; visiting curator at Cornerhouse (now HOME) in Manchester and deputy curator of the Cyprus Pavilion at the 56th Venice Biennale, and is co-founder of the London-based curatorial collective, DAM Projects.

DANIELLE M. PURIFOY

is a writer, lawyer, and current Carolina Postdoctoral Fellow in the Department of Geography at The University of North Carolina at Chapel Hill. She received her J.D. from Harvard Law School and Ph.D. in Environmental Politics and African American Studies from Duke University. Her current research traces the roots of contemporary environmental inequality in the US South, particularly in the development of Black towns and settlements.

Danielle is an editor for Scalawag, a magazine devoted to Southern politics and culture and a board member of the North Carolina Environmental Justice Network.

STAFF LIST

JOHN MCINERNEY
Interim Daniel W. Dietrich, II Director

AMY SADAO
Former Daniel W. Dietrich, II Director

KATE ABERCROMBIE
Registrar

LIZ BARR
Former Public Engagement Assistant

JAMES E. BRITT, JR.
DAJ Director of Public Engagement

ROBERT CHANEY
Marc J. Leder Director of Curatorial Affairs

ELIZABETH CHONG
Visitor Services Coordinator

LAUREN DOWNING
Executive Assistant to the Director

ANTHONY ELMS
Daniel and Brett Sundheim Chief Curator

SHANNON FREITAS
Director of Administration

STEPHANIE GARCIA
Van Doren Engagement Fellow

JESSICA JOHNSON
Former Visitor Services Coordinator

TAJA JONES
Associate Director of Development & Alumni Relations

JES KAMINSKI
Administrative Coordinator

JILL KATZ
Director of Marketing & Communications

DANIELLA ROSE KING
Whitney-Lauder Curatorial Fellow

ALEX KLEIN
Dorothy & Stephen R. Weber (CHE '60) Curator

KATE KRACZON
Former Andrea B. Laporte Associate Curator

ALI ABDEL MOHSEN
Digital Content Editor

TAUSIF NOOR
Spiegel-Wilks Curatorial Fellow

BRUNO NOURIL
Director of Development & Alumni Relations

MEG ONLI
Andrea B. Laporte Associate Curator

CAITLIN PALMER
Curatorial Administrative Coordinator

MICHELE PIERSON
Development Administrative Coordinator

DEREK RIGBY
Audio Visual Coordinator

NATALIE SANDSTROM
Programs Coordinator

PAUL SWENBECK
Chief Preparator & Building Administrator

CHRISTINA YU
Assistant Director of Development & Alumni Relations

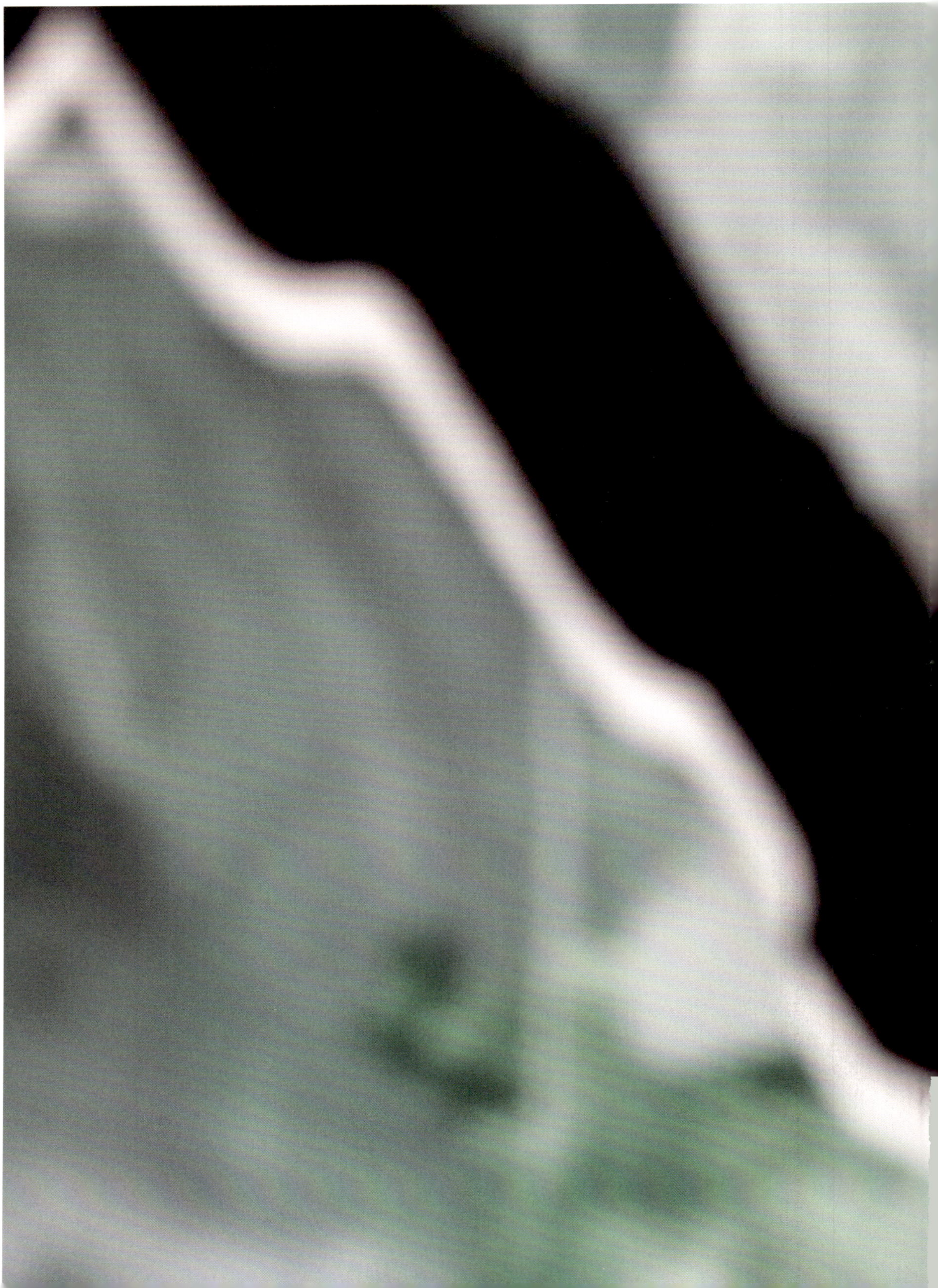

Inhospitable (detail), 2018. Courtesy of the artist.

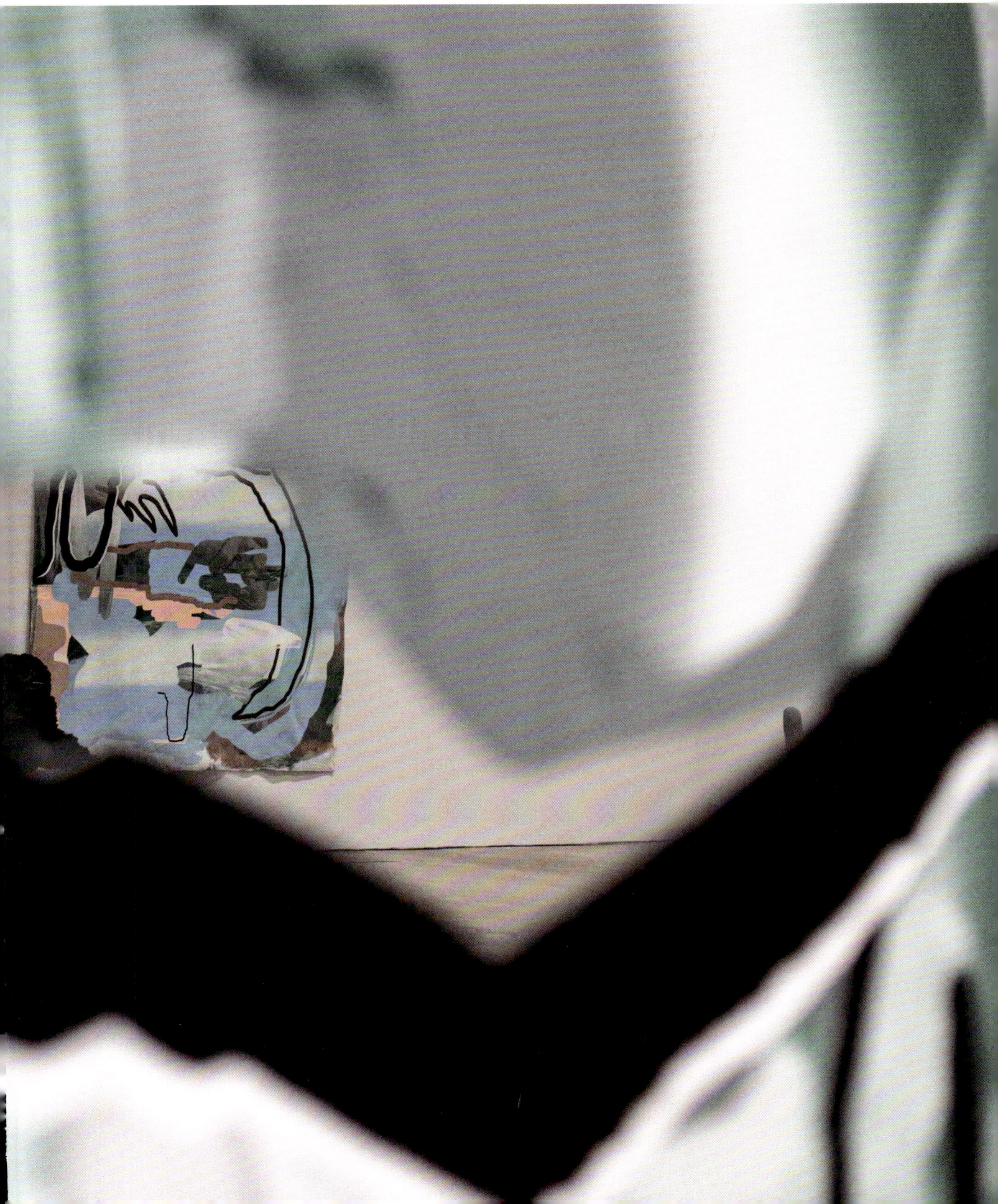

COLOPHON

This book is published on the occasion of the exhibition *Deborah Anzinger: An Unlikely Birth*, curated by Daniella Rose King, Whitney-Lauder Curatorial Fellow 2017–2020, and organized and presented by the Institute of Contemporary Art, University of Pennsylvania, April 26–August 11, 2019.

Support for this exhibition and for ICA's Whitney-Lauder Curatorial Fellow Program has been provided by the Leonard & Judy Lauder Fund.

Editor
DANIELLA ROSE KING

Additional editing and copy editing
JONATHAN SMITH
DAVID UPDIKE

Design
NONTSIKELELO MUTITI

Photography
CONSTANCE MENSH

Printing
DIE KEURE

Typeface
Joly Romyn designed by
WEI HUANG

First Edition
Edition of 750
ISBN: 978-088454-152-3

Institute of Contemporary Art
University of Pennsylvania
118 S. 36th Street
Philadelphia, PA 19104-3289
www.icaphila.org

Library of Congress Cataloging-in-Publication Data
CIP data can be obtained at the Library of Congress

ICA is always Free. For All. Free admission is courtesy of Amanda and Glenn Fuhrman.

ICA acknowledges the generous sponsorship of Barbara B. & Theodore R. Aronson for exhibition publications. Programming at ICA has been made possible in part by the Emily and Jerry Spiegel Fund to Support Contemporary Culture and Visual Arts and the Lise Spiegel Wilks and Jeffrey Wilks Family Foundation, and by Hilarie L. & Mitchell Morgan. Marketing is supported by Pamela Toub Berkman & David J. Berkman, Catherine O'Connor Carrafiell & John Carrafiell, and by Brett & Daniel Sundheim. Public Engagement is supported by the Bernstein Public Engagement Fund. Exhibitions at ICA are supported by Stephanie & David Simon. Additional funding has been provided by The Horace W. Goldsmith Foundation, the Overseers Board for the Institute of Contemporary Art, friends and members of ICA, and the University of Pennsylvania. General operating support is provided, in part, by the Philadelphia Cultural Fund.
ICA receives state arts funding

support through a grant from the Pennsylvania Council on the Arts, a state agency funded by the Commonwealth of Pennsylvania and the National Endowment for the Arts, a federal agency.

ARTS pennsylvania
COUNCIL ON THE ARTS

The Philadelphia Cultural Fund